The American Dietetic Association Association Guide to Healthy Eating for Kids

The American Dietetic Association Guide to Healthy Eating for Kids

◆ ◆ ◆

HOW YOUR CHILDREN CAN EAT SMART FROM FIVE TO TWELVE

Jodie Shield, M.Ed., R.D.
Mary Catherine Mullen, M.S., R.D.

JOHN WILEY & SONS, INC.

Published by John Wiley & Sons, Inc., Hoboken, New Jersey
Published simultaneously in Canada

Design and production by Navta Associates, Inc.

This publication is designed to provide accurate and authoritative information in regard to the subject matter covered. It is sold with the understanding that the publisher is not engaged in rendering professional services. If professional advice or other expert assistance is required, the services of a competent professional person should be sought.

ISBN 0-471-44224-0

Printed in the United States of America

10 9 8 7 6 5 4 3 2

Contents

◆ ◆ ◆

Foreword

◆ ◆ ◆

Shortly after I returned home from China with my adopted daughter, Eleni, I received a visit from my friend and colleague Jodie Shield. Jodie had come to help me—a bewildered first-time parent—learn the nuances of motherhood and, most important, figure out how to feed my very hungry nine-month-old child. Well, over the course of a weekend, Jodie introduced Eleni to mashed potatoes, flavored yogurt, ripe bananas, and other healthful American favorites, and as each new food approached my daughter's high-chair tray, her eyes widened with curiosity, interest, and delight.

These days, Eleni is no longer a baby, and my "big girl" (who still eats her fruits and veggies) will soon be going to school. Before long, she'll be racing for the school bus, swapping lunches in the cafeteria, going to birthday parties and friends' houses, and making food choices of her own. And as much as I'd always like to be there, my daughter will be growing up and spreading her nutritional wings. That's why I'm grateful to Jodie Shield and Mary Mullen— registered dietitians with seven school-age children between them—for having written *Healthy Eating for Kids*, a modern-day bible for busy, health-conscious families. In the following pages, you'll find practical, friendly advice on all aspects of raising a healthy eater—and, most important, you'll learn how to teach your child to make sound decisions on her own. I think of this book as a personal visit from a registered dietitian. I know that you will too.

—Laura Broadwell
Former editor, *Healthy Kids* magazine

Acknowledgments

❖ ❖ ❖

I would like to thank my parents for the family meals we've shared; my partner and friend, Mary Mullen, for putting up with me all of these years; my husband, Jim, and our three children, Jennifer, J.J., and Michael, for teaching me the "true" meaning of healthy eating; and all of my editors and publishers, especially Laura Broadwell, for allowing me to spread the news about eating smart.

—Jodie Shield, M.Ed., R.D.

Thanks to my family for their patience, encouragement, and love—especially my husband, Joe, and my children, Joseph, Kevin, Anne, and Maura. Thanks to my family, friends, and clients who offered practical advice and shared their real-life experiences. Thanks to Laura Broadwell for sharing her editorial expertise and guidance, and Diana Faulhaber for her support and publishing wisdom. And last, thanks to Jodie for making this book become a reality.

—Mary Mullen, M.S., R.D.

Introduction

An Orientation to Eating Smart

◆   ◆   ◆

How often do you think your grade-schooler eats his or her lunch? Before you answer, let me share a little story with you. Last year when I was helping out in my kids' school cafeteria, I overheard a couple of first-graders involved in a high-stakes nutrition negotiation. The deal went down something like this:

> Michael: "I'll trade you my apple for your chips."
> Tyler: "Not unless you give me your cookies, your juice box, *and* your salami sandwich."
> Michael: "All right, you've got a deal."

Much to my surprise (and personal horror), the nutritional loser who traded his entire lunch for a bag of chips was my very own son, Michael!

As a fellow parent of a grade-schooler you may not want to believe it, but trades like these go on all of the time. When your child was a preschooler, you had control over most of the foods he ate. But during the grade school years, your child will be making many of his *own* food choices—at school, at friends' houses, at parties—without you around. Will he be selecting nutritious foods or loading up on

1

fatty, sugary treats? The answer depends on the efforts of *both* of you. Raising healthy eaters, just like raising report-card grades, requires a partnership between the parent and the child. As registered dietitians of the American Dietetic Association with more than twenty years of professional experience in the field of childhood nutrition, we believe that the grade school years are the ideal time for you to begin shifting some of the responsibility of healthy eating off your shoulders, and onto your son's or daughter's. By high school, it's too late, because eating habits are set. We've written this book combining both our scientific training as dietitians and our real-life experience as mothers (collectively, we have seven kids, six of whom are still in grade school!). It's our goal that, after reading this book, you will possess all of the nutrition knowledge and practical skills you'll need to teach your child how to eat smart in and out of the classroom, now, and for the rest of his life.

NOT ALL GRADE-SCHOOLERS WERE CREATED EQUAL

Unlike other children's nutrition books, which lump all kids from preschoolers to teenagers together, we've written this book specifically focusing on children in kindergarten through sixth grade. That's because as dietitians, we know the grade school years are nutritionally a very important time for children. In fact, during these years your child will have grown on average between one and two feet, and doubled her weight. In addition, we've divided our advice into the early grade school years (ages five through eight) and the later grade school years (ages nine through twelve). Why? Well, there are two key reasons. First of all, at around age nine children's requirements for *all* nutrients increase dramatically to support their growth and development for puberty. Secondly, as mothers we understand that between the ages of five and twelve, children's appetites and food preferences change radically. My coauthor, Mary, experienced this firsthand with her kids. She discovered that her second-grade daughter, Anne, was far more interested in recess than eating lunch, and often brought her lunch box home untouched, while her sixth-grade son, Joseph, frequently complained that he never had enough time, or lunch, to eat. By segmenting grade school into the early and later years we will be able to provide you with more age-specific nutrition and feeding recommendations to share with your child.

IF YOUR FAMILY IS ON THE GO, THIS BOOK IS FOR YOU!

As mothers of very socially and academically active children, we know how busy you are and that feeding your child during the grade school years can be a challenge. If your family is like ours you may be struggling with some of the following situations:

The Breakfast Crunch. You're late for a meeting and the school bus leaves at 7:00 A.M. Who has time for breakfast? It's no wonder that 12 percent of all grade school kids start their day without a morning meal.

The Lunch Exchange. What you send to eat rarely ends up in your child's stomach. In fact, on any given day, one out of four kids trades—or tosses—his lunch. That's because the cafeteria is really the Board of Trade and lunch is a "hot" commodity.

The Dine-and-Dash Dinner. Whether it's fast food eaten en route to soccer practice, or frozen dinners and carry-out meals gobbled down at home, families want dinner on the table in thirty minutes or less.

The Couch Potato Kid. Besides the fact that kids are making some unwise food choices, they're not running around and playing as much. The most popular sport seems to be surfing, not at the beach, but through TV channels or on the Internet. Less than

25 percent of grade school kids get the recommended sixty minutes of physical activity every day.

Our book will give you hands-on, practical advice about how to turn these, and many other dilemmas, into fun, nutrition-education opportunities. Your child will learn how to make wise food choices in a variety of eating situations—in the school cafeteria, at a fast-food restaurant, even during a birthday party. And she will understand why eating healthfully can help her perform better on tests as well as on the playing field.

HOW TO USE THIS BOOK

While we certainly encourage you to read *all* of the book, we understand that you're a busy parent, and that time is a precious commodity. To help you get the most out of this book, and spend your valuable time wisely, we've written the book in a format so that it can serve as a reference for you throughout your child's grade school years. Each chapter can stand on its own and identifies other sections of the book that may also be helpful to you. That way you can find the information you want quickly. It's our hope that whenever you have a concern about your child's eating habits, you'll be able to pick up this book and turn immediately to the chapter and sections that address your concern, and more importantly, find a solution that works for you and your child.

Each chapter is actually a lively and exciting crash course in nutrition based on the latest scientific research. You'll find reader-friendly summaries of the latest nutrition studies; practical feeding suggestions, recipes and menus; and answers to questions most frequently asked by parents of grade school–age kids.

But are you ready for the best part? At the end of each chapter you'll find optional "extra-credit" assignments for you and your child to work on together. Don't worry, these won't take up much of your time, because they can easily be incorporated into your daily routine. (In fact, they may actually *save* you time!)

GETTING STARTED

So where should you begin? If you've got the time, start with Chapter 1. If not, the following chart can help you identify where to start reading by pinpointing "red-flag" or problem areas in your child's diet. Whether you choose to jump around or read the book from cover to cover, we are confident that you and your child will graduate from this book knowing how to boost your nutritional grades and understanding what it means to eat smart.

Problem Areas at a Glance . . . Which Ones Apply to Your Child?

Take a look at each of the red-flag eating problems below. If any of the traits sound familiar, your child's diet could probably use some help in that particular area.

Is your child a . . . ?	Trait	Then go to:
Bossy or Unreasonable Eater	• Thinks you're a short-order cook • Prefers candy to cauliflower • Believes foods that are good for you couldn't possibly taste good	Chapter 1: *Feeding Kids Philosophy 101*
Nutritionally Clueless Nibbler	• Thinks the Food Pyramid is a building in Egypt • Can name only two out of the five food groups • Thinks you mine for minerals • Would rather take a vitamin pill than eat a vegetable	Chapter 2: *Nutrition Fundamentals*

(continued)

Is your child a . . . ?	Trait	Then go to:
Breakfast Skipper or Skimper	• Frequently skips breakfast • Is not hungry early in the morning • Has no time for breakfast • Eats only sugary cereals or doughnuts • Wouldn't think of making her own breakfast	Chapter 3: *Breakfast for Brain Power*
Lunchroom Trasher or Trader	• Brings home uneaten lunch • Trades lunch frequently • Claims to not like hot lunch at school • Tends to eat the same thing every day • Doesn't make his own lunch	Chapter 4: *Lessons on Lunch*
Snack-a-holic	• Prefers snacking to eating meals • Is too busy after school for a snack • Snacks on chips and sodas • Can't prepare her own snacks • Buys snacks from school vending machines	Chapter 6: *After-School Snack Attacks*
Dine-and-Dash Dinner Partner	• Has no time for a sit-down family meal • Eats lots of frozen dinners • Eats in front of the TV set • Is not involved in menu planning • Doesn't know how to cook • Has never learned how to set the table	Chapter 5: *Family Dinners in a Flash*
Concession-Stand Connoisseur	• Is surrounded by treats all day long (classroom parties, Scout meetings, sporting events, etc.)	Chapter 7: *Extracurricular Eating*

Is your child a...?	Trait	Then go to:
Concession-Stand Connoisseur *(continued)*	• Can't resist giant-size movie theater popcorn • Loves eating fast food • Thinks the best thing about birthday parties is the cake, ice cream, and candy goody bag • Lives on hot dogs and nachos over summer vacation • Believes Halloween candy rocks	Chapter 7: *Extracurricular Eating*
Cooking Illiterate	• Prefers reading the cartoons on cereal boxes rather than the food label • Thinks washing hands once a day is enough • Can't find the fresh produce section in the supermarket • Believes that the wok is a new rock band	Chapter 8: *Culinary Kids*
Remote-Control Athlete	• Can't stand gym class • Watches more than two hours of TV a day • Prefers playing video sports games to actually playing the sport • Spends more time on the computer than outdoors playing	Chapter 9: *A Moving Subject*
Risky Eater	• Wants to be a vegetarian • Worries about weight • Has no concerns about fat and cholesterol • Eats only organic foods • Has food allergies • Seems hyperactive after eating sugar	Chapter 10: *Red Flags*

CHAPTER 1

Feeding Kids Philosophy 101

◆ ◆ ◆

I eat foods 'cause they're yummy.
—MARQUITA, FIRST GRADE

If I eat three peas can I have dessert?
—TAYLOR, THIRD GRADE

Why can't I drink soda? You do.
—BRIAN, SIXTH GRADE

Top Three Mistakes Parents Make When Feeding Grade-Schoolers:

1. Resort to bribery to force kids to eat.
2. Offer giant-sized portions.
3. Let kids eat whatever they want.

During the grade school years kids say, and eat, the darnedest things. For most parents it appears as though their child is constantly testing their patience. But what they're really looking for are limits. "How late can I stay up?" "Can I have my ears pierced?" "Why do I have to drink milk?" Hang in there, especially when it comes to eating, because your child's future health depends on it. In this chapter you'll:

- discover why most kids would rather eat candy than cauliflower;
- learn how to divide eating responsibilities and develop a "gold-star" feeding relationship with your child;
- find out what motivates grade-schoolers to learn about nutrition and healthy eating.

WHO'S PRINCIPALLY IN CHARGE OF EATING?

Looking back on the preschool years, it seems that feeding your child was a breeze. While you may have experienced a few food jags (your child wanting to eat the same food for weeks) or some picky-eater tantrums, overall you felt as though you were in control of your child's eating. But now that your child is in grade school, you may be feeling out of control, or at the very least that you're losing it. Bus routes, school schedules, and extracurricular activities seem to be dictating your child's breakfast, lunch, and dinner choices. But don't let the competition catch you off guard. You, the parent, are still chiefly in charge of your child's eating.

Our colleague, Ellyn Satter (who happens to be a dietitian, social worker, and mother), has spent years studying the feeding relationship and control issues between parents and children of all ages. Her approach to feeding kids is supported by years of nutrition research, and she calls it the division of feeding responsibilities. We feel her approach is the *key* to raising a child who can eat smart. Let's begin by examining who's responsible for what in this feeding relationship.

The Division of Feeding Responsibilities

1. *Parents are responsible for the what, when, and where of feeding.* In other words, *what* types of foods are offered (nutritious),

when they're offered (at regularly scheduled times), and *where* they're offered (at home or outside of the home).

2. *Children are responsible for the how much and the whether of eating.* How much he's going to eat, or *whether* he's going to eat anything at all.

It may surprise you to find out that children are born with the ability to self-regulate their energy needs (calories). In other words, they instinctively know *how much* they need to eat. Several studies have confirmed that kids, particularly under the age of five, can regulate their daily calorie needs from meal to meal with great consistency. However, studies have also found that when parents try to force or bribe their children into eating, or if they feed their kids extremely large portions, they actually are teaching them to overeat. That's because what the kids are really learning is to ignore their internal cues that tell them to stop eating when they're full.

However, numerous studies have found that while kids can regulate the *quantity* of what they eat, they can't regulate the *quality* of what they consume. Parents need to realize that children are born with a natural preference for sweet tastes. Given the choice between a piece of candy or a carrot stick, kids are internally wired to take the sweeter deal. In fact, some of the earliest nutrition studies found that when kids were offered a variety of nutritious foods, they were able to select on their own and eat a nutritionally balanced diet. But when sugary foods like candy and soda were also offered, kids frequently choose those foods over the more nutritious foods, and their diets were less balanced.

As the parent of a grade-schooler, if you understand that your role in feeding your child begins and ends with the *what, when,* and *where* of eating, and that you must trust your child to determine *how much* and *whether* he'll eat, you will both be on your way to developing a healthy relationship with food. And that means not teaching your child that more is always better.

Are You Teaching Your Child Portion Distortion?

If you let him order super-size meals or triple-scoop ice cream cones, you just might be. A study, published in the *Journal of the American Dietetic Association,* adds support to the recommendation of offering kids smaller-sized servings. Researchers from Pennsylvania State University served three- and five-year-old kids small, medium, and large portions of macaroni and cheese. The more macaroni and cheese the five-year-olds were offered, the more they ate. Not so for the three-year-olds, who consistently ate the same amount of macaroni and cheese, no matter how much they were offered. Intuitively, the younger children knew what was right for them.

Here's how you can help your child downsize portions and get a better value on her health:

- Order small or regular-size items when eating at a restaurant.
- Read the food label, and offer your child the serving size listed on the package.
- Serve meals family style, and let your child serve himself. Let him take more food only if he wants it.
- Be a role model for your child, and make sure your own portions are not too hefty.

Is There Really Such a Thing as a "Sweet Tooth?"

"Absolutely," says taste researcher Valerie Duffy, Ph.D., R.D., associate professor of dietetics at the University of Connecticut's School of Allied Health, in Storrs. In fact, several studies have found that babies are born craving sweet-tasting foods. But the amount each prefers varies with genetics.

Supertasters, for instance, have more taste buds on their

tongue and need only a small amount of sweetness to satisfy their cravings. On the other hand, nontasters—or those with a so-called sweet tooth—have fewer (not duller) taste buds and need more sweets to curb their cravings.

So what do you do if your child prefers candy to cauliflower? Here's how you can help satisfy your child's sweet tooth:

- Offer foods from the five main food groups of the Food Guide Pyramid before offering foods from the fats, and sweets category (see Chapter 2).
- Entice your child to eat foods by adding fruits to them and sweetening them up. Try adding raisins to oatmeal, mandarin orange sections to salads, and pineapple to stir-fry dishes.
- Reduce the amount of sugar by one-fourth to one-third when baking cookies, cakes, or sweet breads. You can do so without altering the taste.

THE FEEDING RESPONSIBILITIES IN ACTION

Just to make sure that you are perfectly comfortable with the division of feeding responsibilities, let's take a look at how they play out in real-life situations.

During the Early Grade School Years

During the early grade school years the division of feeding responsibilities works rather smoothly because you are still in control of most of your child's food choices. Here's an example of how it can work.

In the morning (*when*), at your house (*where*), you provide your first-grader with a bowl of oatmeal, a glass of low-fat milk, and an orange for breakfast (*what*). Congratulations! You have successfully completed your parental feeding responsibilities. Your daughter decides she's going to drink all of the milk (how much and whether) and eat the orange. Congratulations! She's successfully completed her feeding responsibilities.

Sounds easy enough, but what about the oatmeal? While it's unfortunate that she chose not to eat it, remember that's her call to make. But as the parent, it now becomes your responsibility to make sure that you offer her another opportunity throughout the day to eat a grain group food (which is where oatmeal fits into the Food Guide Pyramid: see Chapter 2). Better yet, talk with your daughter and discuss why she needs to eat foods from the grain group, and together brainstorm other foods you could offer for breakfast that she would be willing to eat.

During the Later Grade School Years

As your child graduates to the upper grades, the line dividing your feeding responsibilities and those of your child will become hazy at times. The responsibilities will begin to shift and need to be shared since she'll be eating many more foods outside of the home at places like school, sporting events, and friends' houses. In other words, your child will occasionally be responsible for the *what*, *when*, and *where*.

Having experienced this shift in shared responsibilities with our own children, we can guarantee you that there will be times when you'll be less than thrilled with some of your child's food choices. Relax, this is a normal part of your child's growing up. But do realize that how you handle these eating situations will ultimately teach your child how to eat smart. Our advice is to remain focused on the feeding relationship and the original division of feeding responsibilities. As the parent, you are still in charge of mealtimes (*when*) and the foods (*what*) that you bring into your home (*where*). For example, if you know that your fifth-grader will be consuming fatty chips or sugary soft drinks at a friend's house, then make sure that those foods are not available in your home. Or if your sixth-grader buys candy at an after-school volleyball game and turns her nose up at dinner, don't bother to scold her. Instead, remind her that if she plans on eating candy, then she must eat it earlier in the day or have a smaller amount so that it won't spoil her appetite for dinner.

HOW TO DEVELOP A GOLD-STAR FEEDING RELATIONSHIP

We understand that our philosophy of feeding kids and the dual responsibility of the feeding relationship may seem radical at first, but it *does* work. However, in order for it to work successfully for you and your child, you must accept the following three points:

- *There's no such thing as a perfect diet.* A day or week of poor food choices will not make or break your child's diet. It's the type of foods he eats over time that will eventually affect his health. For example, if your child indulges in Halloween candy for a week, he's not going to become overweight. But if he indulges in candy every day and doesn't get enough physical activity, then he eventually may have problems with his weight.
- *Mistakes are okay.* As parents we want what's best for our children, and it's tempting to try to control everything to shelter them from the pain of failure. But we can assure you, if you want your child to grow up and eat smart, you'll need to let him experiment and make mistakes *now* while he's in grade school. Using our example from before, if he chooses to eat too many pieces of Halloween candy and gets a tummy ache, ideally he'll learn to think twice about pigging out on candy the next time. As a rule of thumb, remember that every time you try to control or take over your child's feeding responsibilities, you're denying your child an opportunity to grow and learn. In addition, you may be setting him up for future eating problems and disorders, such as obesity or anorexia (see Chapter 10).
- *Actions speak louder than words.* If you want your child to grow up and eat smart, the most important thing you can do is be a positive role model, and eat smart too. "Practice what you

preach." "Monkey see, monkey do." Both are catch phrases for what decades of scientific research have demonstrated: children learn best by *watching* others. So if you want your child to drink milk, fill up a glass for yourself and bottoms up. Or if you want your child to be more physically active, turn off the TV and take the dog for a long walk. Also, don't be discouraged if your child doesn't follow your good example right away. It takes time, and often maturity, before you see results. Your job now is to plant the seeds by serving and eating nutritious foods, then patiently wait for your good example to grow.

TUNING IN TO YOUR GRADE-SCHOOLER'S LEARNING POTENTIAL

Before you can begin helping your child learn how to eat smart, it's important to understand where your child is intellectually, socially, and emotionally, because he will change throughout the grade school years. Here are some of the key developmental highlights for both younger and older grade-schoolers, along with some tips for teaching kids about nutrition.

The Early Grade School Child (Kindergarten through Third Grade)

Intellectually. Younger grade-schoolers are in what educators call the preoperations period of development. They are not yet capable of thinking logically, such as realizing that eating a carton of low-fat yogurt would be a healthier snack than a candy bar because it has more nutrients. And they have no real concept of gradual change, such as what they eat now may affect them in the future.

Socially. During the early years of grade school, kids are still basically egocentric. They really don't understand other people's point of view (why mom's upset that they're not eating their vegetables).

And they're less interested in how things work and more interested in how things affect them. Perhaps this is why bribes seem to be so effective at this age: if you don't eat your vegetables then you can't _____ (fill in the blank). But remember, food bribes can and will work against you. Children are smart enough to figure out that if they have to be bribed to eat something, it must be pretty bad. We'll discuss food bribes more in the box that follows in this chapter.

Emotionally. One of the joys of the early grade school years is that kids are very energetic and enthusiastic about learning. But one of the frustrating things is that kids this age are also easily distracted and have trouble finishing things. For example, they may be delighted to select their own cereal on your shopping trip, but forget all about the task at hand if they pass another aisle in the supermarket that has toys.

Nutrition Tips. Here are several strategies aimed at teaching a younger child about nutrition and healthy eating:

- *Pique their interest in food.* Provide your child with a variety of different foods. Ask them to describe them based on color and shape. Or grow a garden and talk about where fruits and vegetables come from and how they are used to prepare foods. Now is the time to introduce kids gradually to the concept of foods belonging to certain food groups (see Chapter 2).
- *Tell them, "Try it, you'll like it."* Children are instinctively fearful of trying new foods. Studies have found that it can take up to eight to ten tries before some kids will even take a bite. Be patient and continue to offer new foods to your child.
- *Encourage kids to help themselves.* Pass foods around the table family style and let your child take their own serving. That way he will learn to be more in control of how much and whether or not to eat.
- *Get them cooking.* Kids have more of an interest in learning, and in eating, if they've played a role in making a meal. Find

age-appropriate ways for your child to help prepare foods such as tossing salads, stirring batter, or spreading peanut butter on bread for sandwiches (see Chapter 8).

Wanted: Vegetables/Reward: Dessert (or: All about Food Bribes)

Many a well-meaning parent has resorted to bribery at times to get their child to eat some type of nutritious food. But according to Dr. Leann Birch and her colleagues at Penn. State University, this approach is destined to backfire.

In the short run, your child will eat the food because you are there to see things through. But when you're not around, don't count on it. That's because studies have found that kids learn to associate foods with experiences—pleasant and not so pleasant. Bribes teach kids that the food they're being bribed to eat must be pretty bad, and the reward food must be very good. The result is that the child actually develops an increased preference for the reward food, and decreased preference for the food you're encouraging them to eat. How can you teach your child to eat and enjoy a variety of nutritious foods? Here are a few strategies:

- Tempt your child's taste buds. Remember that kids eat foods because they taste good, not because they're good for them. Look for ways to prepare foods so that they're more appealing. For example, try serving veggies with a low-fat yogurt dip.
- Be a role model. Make sure that your child sees you eating and enjoying the foods you are trying to entice her to eat.
- Serve desserts with the meal, rather than at the end. That way no single food becomes more important than another.

The Older Grade School Child
(Fourth through Sixth Grades)

Intellectually. During the later grade school years, children progress to the concrete operations period of development. They're more logical in their thinking and ready to have a better understanding of the Food Guide Pyramid and other nutrition information. It's during this time that your child will begin to realize that healthy foods have a positive effect on his growth and health.

Socially. Now is the time when kids are developing a sense of self. They're less egocentric and may even become more of what psychologists call "cognitively conceited"—they think they know more than their parents. Also, friends begin to play an important role, and children can be very influenced by their peers. If your son loves turkey sandwiches, for instance, but the peer culture thinks they're uncool, he may say that he doesn't like them anymore. Your best bet is to let him take food to school that you both agree upon, and save the turkey sandwiches for weekends at home.

Emotionally. During the later grade school years, kids value being independent of their parents. They take pride in doing what their parents ask, such as making their lunch in the morning, and prefer to do it by themselves without close parental supervision. But at the same time, they are looking for, and need, recognition for their actions. Praise your child often by saying things like, "Great job. You packed your lunch!"

Nutrition Tips. Here are just a few of the ways you can get an older grade-schooler interested in learning about nutrition:

- *Take a tour of the pyramid.* Older children are ready to learn about the Food Guide Pyramid and how it can help them learn how to eat smart (see Chapter 2). They are also ready to start learning about different nutrients and the role they play in keeping them healthy.

- *Introduce them to the Dietary Guidelines.* Now is the perfect time to help kids become familiar with the concept that staying healthy entails: A—Aiming for a healthy weight; B—Building a healthy base; and C—Choosing sensibly (see Chapter 2).
- *Be a trendsetter.* Invite your child's peers over for lunch or dinner and let them experience how your family eats. Or send your child to school with several extras of a new or unfamiliar food so that he can share them with friends.
- *Get them more involved in the kitchen.* Kids love to experiment with preparing foods on their own. Teach them how to safely operate equipment, like microwave ovens and blenders. And let them use their imagination to create their own healthy concoctions (see Chapter 8).

EXTRA-CREDIT ASSIGNMENT

Eating Responsibilities Worksheet

How would you like to have a gold-star eating relationship with your child? Complete the following worksheet, and you'll both be on your way to eating smart. First, you fill out the chart on page 22. Then let your child use it as a checklist to keep track of his responsibilities. At the end of the week, evaluate your progress together to make sure that nobody is shirking their responsibilities.

Parent's Feeding Responsibilities—Establish an Eating Game Plan

When: Take a look at your family's schedules and establish regular mealtimes; share these times with your child.

Where: Identify where each of the meals will be eaten.

What: Jot down a menu for each day's meals (see Chapters 3 through 6).

Child's Responsibilities—Follow the Eating Game Plan

How much and whether or not to eat: Place a check mark by each meal that you: (1) came to hungry and ready to eat, and (2) if you made selections *only from the foods being offered.* In other words, you didn't sneak into the refrigerator or pantry and help yourself to something else.

Reviewing the Eating Game Plan

Parents: Did you successfully complete your feeding responsibilities? If not, why? How would you revise the game plan for the next time?

Child: Did you successfully complete your feeding responsibilities? If not, why? What might you try to help you follow the game plan the next time?

Eating Game Plan

TIME & PLACE	MONDAY	TUESDAY	WEDNESDAY	THURSDAY	FRIDAY	SATURDAY	SUNDAY
Breakfast Time____ Place____							
Lunch Time____ Place____							
Snack Time____ Place____							
Dinner Time____ Place____							

CHAPTER 2

Nutrition
*Fun*damentals

◆　◆　◆

Name the food groups? Easy: pizza, pop, candy, and cookies.
　　　　　　　　　　　　　　　—JOSEPH, SIXTH GRADE

The only way I'll eat broccoli is smothered in ketchup.
　　　　　　　　　　　　　　　—KENT, THIRD GRADE

"Mommy says too much sugar makes me hyper."
　　　　　　　　　　　　　　　—JEAN, FIRST GRADE

**Top Three Things Parents Don't
Understand about Nutrition:**

1. There's no such thing as a "good" or "bad" food.
2. How to actually use the Food Guide Pyramid.
3. Never heard of the U.S. Dietary Guidelines.

If you've been on a quest, searching for the best way to feed your grade-schooler, you've reached your destination. After reading this chapter you'll know more about what your child should be eating throughout the grade school years, and more importantly, how to actually get her to eat it. In this chapter you'll:

- explore the Food Guide Pyramid from the bottom to the top;
- learn the ABCs of the Dietary Guidelines and how they can improve your child's future health;
- discover strategies for teaching your child about the Food Guide Pyramid and the Dietary Guidelines.

EXPLORING THE PYRAMIDS

If your child thinks the Food Guide Pyramid is a monument in Egypt, he is not alone. Many children don't know what the United States Department of Agriculture's (USDA) Food Guide Pyramid is, and many don't come close to eating the recommended daily servings of food from each of the five main food groups. In fact, a recent government survey found that kids are flunking healthy eating. Only 2 percent of kids today meet all of the Food Guide Pyramid requirements, and 16 percent do not meet any of the requirements at all.

But the Food Guide Pyramid is only half of the healthy-eating equation. Healthy eating and physical activity must go hand in hand. While it's important for kids to eat a variety of nutritious foods, equal emphasis must be placed on getting kids to become more physically active. You can teach your child more about healthy eating, and the importance of physical activity, by exploring the pyramids. Let's take a tour of the Food Guide Pyramid now because it can help your child learn how to make healthier food choices. In Chapter 9 we will explore the Kid's Activity Pyramid, which can help your child be more physically active. Together, both pyramids hold the secrets to living healthfully ever after.

DIG IN TO THE FOOD GUIDE PYRAMID

Hardly ancient history, the USDA's Food Guide Pyramid was first released in 1992 and is a direct ancestor of the Basic Four Food

Food Guide Pyramid

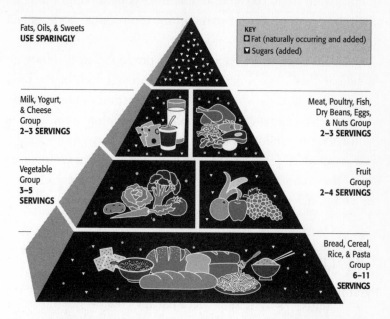

The Food Guide Pyramid. *U.S. Department of Agriculture and the U.S. Department of Health and Human Services*

Groups: bread, milk, meat, and fruits/vegetables. It was developed so that children and adults could have a handy way to visualize what healthy eating looked like.

The pyramid shape and the position of food groups reflect how the diet should be balanced: *most* food selections should come from the base of the pyramid, which contains nutrient-rich, grain-based foods, vegetables, and fruits; *some* food selections should come from the middle section of the pyramid, which is where you'll find dairy and protein-rich foods, like meat, fish, and poultry; and *fewer* food selections should come from the tip of the pyramid, which is where you'll find foods with lots of calories but few if any nutrients. Each day your child should eat at least the *minimum* number of recommended servings from each food group. One exception is the dairy group. Because children's bones need a great deal of calcium, kids, especially during the later grade school years (around age nine), should try to consume at least three daily servings from this group (see Appendix A for more information about nutrients and their specific functions).

A key message of the Food Guide Pyramid is that there are no "good" or "bad" foods. So as you scan through each of the food groups, you'll notice a wide range of food selections—some that are even high in fat and sugar! That's because in addition to *balance*, the Food Guide Pyramid teaches the concepts of *variety*, or eating a wide selection of foods within each food group, and *moderation*, or eating the recommended amounts of foods that correspond to a child's age, size, and activity level (see chart that follows).

What Counts as a Serving?

Bread, Cereal, Rice, and Pasta Group (Grains Group)—
whole grain and refined

   1 slice bread

   about 1 cup ready-to-eat cereal (1 ounce)

   ½ cup of cooked cereal, rice, or pasta

Vegetable Group

   1 cup of raw leafy vegetables, such as lettuce or spinach

   ½ cup of other vegetables—cooked or raw

   ¾ cup of vegetable juice

Fruit Group

   1 medium apple, banana, orange, pear

   ½ cup of chopped, cooked, or canned fruit

   ¾ cup of fruit juice

Milk, Yogurt, and Cheese Group (Dairy Group)

   1 cup of milk or yogurt

   1½ ounces of natural cheese (such as cheddar)

   2 ounces of processed cheese (such as American)

Meat, Poultry, Fish, Dry Beans, Eggs, and Nuts Group (Protein Group)

2–3 ounces of cooked lean meat, poultry, or fish

½ cup of cooked dry beans counts as 1 ounce of lean meat

1 egg counts as 1 ounce of lean meat

2 tablespoons of peanut butter counts as 1 ounce of meat

TAKING A CLOSER LOOK AT EACH OF THE FOOD GROUPS

In the next section of this chapter, you will learn more about the Dietary Guidelines, which can help you fine-tune some of your child's food choices. But for now, here's a general overview of each of the food groups.

Grains Group. Some examples: bread, cereal, rice, pasta, English muffins, pancakes, waffles, doughnuts, croissants, hamburger buns, crackers, pretzels, popcorn, rice cakes, tortillas, cookies, pies and cakes.

Foods in this group provide carbohydrates, which serve as your child's main energy source, and several B-complex vitamins, which act like spark plugs and help your child's body use the energy. Whole-grain foods from this group (whole-wheat bread, oatmeal, brown rice) will also provide fiber that can help regulate bowel movements. Kids usually love foods from this food group, but here are a few things to try to help them get more variety:

- Serve sandwiches on different types of bread like pita, rye, or whole-grain.
- Experiment with grains like couscous or quinoa (a small bead-shaped grain that cooks like rice) and different-shaped pastas.
- Rotate the types of cereal you buy, or mix several types together for a quick trail mix.

Vegetable Group. Some examples: broccoli, carrots, green beans, peas, lettuce, and potatoes.

Vegetables, in general, provide a wide variety of vitamins and minerals. In addition, dark yellow or deep green veggies like squash or spinach are excellent sources of vitamin A, which can help keep skin healthy, improve night vision, and boost the immune system.

With the exception of french fries and potato chips, this food group is the least popular for most kids, so it's important to encourage your child to be adventurous with vegetables. Here are a few tricks that will have them nibbling in no time.

- Serve lightly steamed broccoli spears or bell pepper strips with a yogurt dip.
- Add grated or chopped veggies to pasta sauces, soups, or stews.
- Cook vegetables like carrots in broth for added flavor.

Fruit Group. Some examples: apples, bananas, papaya, oranges, melons, and 100 percent fruit juice.

Like vegetables, fruits provide a great deal of vitamins and minerals. Citrus fruits like oranges and grapefruit provide vitamin C, which helps wounds heal and possibly boosts the immune system. Most children love fruit, so go ahead and give it to them. Here are a few fruit-serving tips.

- Mix 100 percent fruit juice with sparkling water for a refreshing juice spritzer.
- Spread peanut butter on apple or pear slices.
- Buy canned fruits like peaches or pineapple packed in natural juice rather than sweetened syrup.

Dairy Group. Some examples: milk, yogurt, cheese, chocolate milk, cottage cheese, pudding, ice cream, and frozen yogurt.

Foods in this group provide bone-building calcium, protein, and carbohydrates and fat for energy. But unfortunately, only 30 percent of school-age children meet their daily dairy requirement. Here are some ways to help your child meet his food-group goal.

- Pour low-fat cheese sauce over broccoli or cauliflower.
- Pack string cheese in you child's lunch for a tasty treat.
- Dunk graham crackers or vanilla wafers in low-fat chocolate milk.

Protein Group. Some examples: meat, poultry, fish, dry beans, nuts, ground beef, pork chops, chicken, turkey, refried beans, tuna fish, hot dogs, eggs, and peanut butter.

Protein is the key nutrient provided by this food group, and your child needs protein in order to grow properly. With such a variety of foods to choose from, it's usually not a problem to meet your child's daily requirements. Here's how to get started.

- Keep hard-boiled eggs handy in the refrigerator.
- Serve red bean chili with a slice of warm bread for a hearty dinner.
- Wrap melon balls with thin slices of turkey or ham, and serve as snack.

Fats, Oils, and Sweets Category. Some examples: salad dressings, jam, syrup, bacon, fruit drinks, soda, and candy.

Technically speaking, this is a category, not a food group. That's because these foods provide little, if any, nutrients, but lots of calories. The reason this category is included in the Food Guide Pyramid is because all foods, even foods like soda and candy, have their place in a healthy diet. It's best to offer foods from this category sparingly, and only once your child has met her daily requirements from each of the other food groups.

FOOD PYRAMID JR.

While the Food Guide Pyramid is appropriate for the older grade school child, some of the concepts may be too difficult for younger grade-schoolers to grasp. That's why the USDA came out with a more kid-friendly version of its original Food Guide Pyramid called the Food Guide Pyramid for Young Children. This pyramid was specifically designed for children between the ages of two and six

FOOD Guide PYRAMID
for Young Children

A Daily Guide for 2- to 6-Year-Olds

Fats & Sweets — **Eat Less**

MILK Group 2 servings

MEAT Group 2 servings

VEGETABLE Group 3 servings

FRUIT Group 2 servings

GRAIN Group 6 servings

U.S. Department of Agriculture
Center for Nutrition Policy and Promotion

January 2000
Program Aid 1651

USDA is an equal opportunity provider and employer.

FOOD IS FUN and learning about food is fun, too. Eating foods from the Food Guide Pyramid and being physically active will help you grow healthy and strong.

WHAT COUNTS AS ONE SERVING?

GRAIN GROUP
1 slice of bread
½ cup of cooked rice or pasta
½ cup of cooked cereal
1 ounce of ready-to-eat cereal

VEGETABLE GROUP
½ cup of chopped raw or cooked vegetables
1 cup of raw leafy vegetables

FRUIT GROUP
1 piece of fruit or melon wedge
¾ cup of juice
½ cup of canned fruit
¼ cup of dried fruit

MILK GROUP
1 cup of milk or yogurt
2 ounces of cheese

MEAT GROUP
2 to 3 ounces of cooked lean meat, poultry, or fish.
½ cup of cooked dry beans, or 1 egg counts as 1 ounce of lean meat. 2 tablespoons of peanut butter count as 1 ounce of meat.

FATS AND SWEETS
Limit calories from these.

Four- to 6-year-olds can eat these serving sizes. Offer 2- to 3-year-olds less, except for milk. Two- to 6-year-old children need a total of 2 servings from the milk group each day.

EAT a variety of FOODS AND ENJOY!

The Food Guide Pyramid for Young Children. *U.S. Department of Agriculture*

and is similar in concept and appearance to its older relative. The "junior pyramid" still has five food groups, and it still emphasizes eating a variety of foods from each group in moderation. But the changes make it easier for younger kids to recognize certain elements of the pyramid and understand how to use it. So show this pyramid to your child if he's in kindergarten or first grade.

What Does a Serving *Really* Look Like?

If you've been scratching your head trying to figure out how three ounces of lean meat looks or what one and a half ounces of cheese looks like, you're not alone. Here are some visual aids to help you figure out the recommended serving size to feed your child.

½ cup fruit, vegetables, cooked cereal, pasta or rice = small fist

3 ounces cooked meat, poultry, or fish = deck of cards

1 muffin = 1 large egg

1 teaspoon of margarine or butter = 1 thumb tip

2 tablespoons of peanut butter = a golf ball

a small baked potato = a computer mouse

1 pancake or waffle = a 4-inch CD

1 medium apple or orange = a baseball

4 small cookies (like vanilla wafers) = four casino chips

1½ ounces of cheese = 6 dice

—Used with permission from Nov./Dec. 1999 Issue of *Food Insight*, IFIC

A DAY IN THE LIFE OF THE FOOD GUIDE PYRAMID

You want your child to eat healthier, but you're not exactly sure how to get started? Go ahead and use the Food Pyramid as your menu-planning guide. All you have to do is make sure your child eats the recommended number of servings from each of the food groups. Here's a tasty sample menu that meets your child's daily food group requirements along with a dinner recipe that's a snap to prepare.

Breakfast
   silver-dollar pancakes with blueberries and reduced-sugar syrup
   skim milk

Lunch
   cheesy turkey tortilla roll-ups with salsa
   tropical fruit salad
   skim milk

Snack
   banana bread
   100 percent fruit juice

Dinner
   honey & apple catfish (recipe follows)
   baked new potatoes
   green beans
   skim milk
   chocolate ice cream

◆ ◆ ◆

Honey & Apple Catfish
Serves 6

½ cup margarine, divided in half
1 tablespoon lemon juice
4 cooking apples, peeled, cored, and sliced into thin wedges
¼ cup honey
3 catfish fillets (6 ounces each)
¼ cup all-purpose flour
2 egg whites, beaten
2 cups dry bread crumbs
¼ teaspoon cinnamon

Melt ¼ cup margarine in a large skillet. Pour 1 tablespoon lemon juice over the apples and add to the skillet. Cook apples over medium heat until they are tender. Remove from heat, and drizzle honey over the apples. Toss and keep warm by covering with a lid and turning the heat to warm.

Melt the remaining ¼ cup margarine in a skillet over medium heat. Dip the catfish fillets in the flour and shake off any excess. Dip the fillets into the egg whites, and then dip into the bread crumbs. Place the coated fillets in the hot skillet, and cook for about 4 to 6 minutes per side. The fillets should be brown and flake easily with a fork.

Place the fillets on a serving dish and spoon the apples with honey over the top of each fillet; sprinkle with a dash of cinnamon.

◆ ◆ ◆

PUTTING THE PYRAMIDS INTO PERSPECTIVE: THE DIETARY GUIDELINES

While the Food Guide Pyramid can help you and your child select foods on a daily basis, the Dietary Guidelines for Americans can help your child eat healthfully in the long run. Since 1980 the USDA's Department of Health and Human Services has published the Dietary Guidelines, which include ten guidelines that point the way to eating for good health. These guidelines are intended for healthy children (ages two years and older) and adults of any age. To keep the Dietary Guidelines as up-to-date as possible, a panel of nutrition experts reviews them every five years. Check out the following chart to see the most recent Dietary Guidelines, which came out in 2000; they're listed in an ABC format, which makes them easier to follow. Throughout this book, all of the advice that we'll offer will reflect the Dietary Guidelines. But don't overwhelm yourself, or your child, by trying to adopt all of the guidelines at once. We suggest that you prioritize them, and begin with those that are most relevant to your child.

Dietary Guidelines for Americans

A = **Aim For Fitness...**
    Aim for a healthy weight.
    Be physically active each day.

B = **Build a Healthy Base...**
    Let the Pyramid guide your food choices.
    Choose a variety of grains daily, especially whole grains.
    Choose a variety of fruits and vegetables every day.
    Keep foods safe to eat.

C = **Choose Sensibly...**
    Choose a diet that is low in saturated fat and cholesterol and
      moderate in total fat.
    Choose beverages and foods to moderate your intake of sugars.
    Choose and prepare foods with less salt.
    If you drink alcoholic beverages, do so in moderation.

Let's take a closer look at each of the Dietary Guidelines and how they can apply to your child's diet.

A = Aim for Fitness

Aim for a Healthy Weight. During the grade school years, children typically grow slowly and steadily, and their appetite will increase and decrease following growth spurts. As a rule, you can expect your grade-schooler to gain about six and one-half pounds and grow a little more than two inches a year until he begins puberty. Because kids come in all shapes and sizes, there is no single healthy weight. Your best bet is to periodically plot your child's weight and height on a growth chart and see if he's growing consistently (see Appendix B for sample growth charts). Your pediatrician or a dietitian can help you use this information to determine if your child is at an appropriate weight for his height (see Chapter 10). In the meantime, here are a few tips for helping your child aim for a healthy weight:

- Keep in mind that grade-schoolers often grow in spurts. One day, your child may seem thick around the middle; the next thing you know, he's shot up and his pants are too loose and short. This is perfectly normal.
- Compliment your child often about her strong, healthy body. This helps bolster self-esteem and will help her learn how to love and accept her body.
- Talk to your pediatrician or dietitian if you think your child has a weight problem. Grade school is not the time for dieting because kids need calories for energy and growth.

Be Physically Active Each Day. One out of every five kids in our country is overweight. This is partly because they're eating more foods that are high in fat and calories, and partly because they're not as active as in years past. Television and computer games have replaced running around and outdoor play. In fact, studies have shown that the more hours of TV kids watch, the higher their percentage of body fat. Also, the layout of many of our communities are designed so that kids can no longer walk or ride their bikes to school or a friend's house; they must rely on the "mommy taxi" for a ride. Because overweight people are at increased risk for developing myriad health problems, such as diabetes, high blood pressure, heart disease, and arthritis, to name a few, and since studies have found that overweight kids have a greater chance of growing up to be overweight adults, it's important to teach your child how to eat nutritiously and exercise regularly. The Dietary Guidelines recommend that kids get at least sixty minutes of physical activity every day (see Chapter 9). Here are a few tips on how you can encourage your child to turn off the screen and turn him on to becoming more physically fit.

- Limit TV viewing and computer time to a total of two hours or less per day. Keep in mind that grade-schoolers, on average, watch four hours of TV a day.
- Take your child to a local playground or indoor gym on the weekends. Or sign her up for an organized activity like dance class or swimming lessons.
- Let your child see that you enjoy being physically active. Walk the dog, rake leaves, or take up a sport like tennis.

B = Build a Healthy Base

Let the Food Pyramid Guide Your Food Choices. The USDA Food Guide Pyramid is a tool you can use to help your child select a balanced diet on a *daily* basis (this was covered earlier in this chapter). The Dietary Guidelines take the Food Guide Pyramid a step further by focusing *more* on specific foods, such as whole grains, vegetables, and fruits, and fine-tuning food selections in each of the food groups in terms of fat, sugar, and sodium contents.

Choose a Variety of Grains Daily, Especially Whole Grains. The majority of your child's food selections should come from the base of the Food Guide Pyramid (the bread, cereal, rice, and pasta group), which is where you'll find whole-grain foods. Numerous studies have found that eating whole-grain foods, which contain dietary fiber, may help ward off future diseases like heart disease or cancer. There are basically two types of dietary fiber: insoluble fiber and soluble fiber. Insoluble fiber, which is found in the bran of whole-grain breads and cereals, can help prevent your child from being constipated and help him feel full and satisfied after eating. Soluble fiber, which is found in oatmeal, beans, fruits, and vegetables, helps lower blood-cholesterol levels and balance out blood-sugar levels.

How much fiber does your child need? The current recommendation is to eat a combination of both types of fiber, and it's easy to remember—it's your child's age plus five grams. So if your child is ten, she should eat fifteen grams of fiber a day. Check out the following chart to learn what foods are high in fiber and how much fiber they contain. Also, here are a few ways to help your child eat more whole-grain foods. Aim for at least three each day.

- Switch to whole-grain breads and crackers, brown rice, and whole-wheat pasta.
- Mix whole-grain cereals with your child's favorite cereal.
- Toss mild-tasting beans like pinto or black beans into soups, salads, and stews.
- Serve a hot bowl of oatmeal in the morning for breakfast.

High-Fiber Food Chart

	Grams of Fiber
Grain Group	
½ cup oatmeal	2
1 slice whole-wheat bread	2
1 cup bran cereal	4
Vegetable Group	
½ cup cooked peas	4
½ cup raw carrots	2.5
Fruit Group	
½ cup strawberries	2
1 medium apple	3.5
Protein Group	
½ cup canned kidney beans	11
½ cup canned pinto beans	5.5
⅓ cup peanuts	4

Choose a Variety of Fruits and Vegetables Daily. The Food Guide Pyramid recommends that children eat a total of at least five servings of vegetables and fruits every day. But surveys have found that 9 percent of kids ages six to eleven are not meeting their five-a-day requirement and are consuming an average of only two and a half servings a day. This is unfortunate since vegetables and fruits offer a cornucopia of vitamins and minerals. Plus, vegetables and fruits along with whole-grains contain phytonutrients (also known as phytochemicals) which are substances found in plants, which studies are beginning to reveal play a role in preventing disease and promoting health. Because no single vegetable or fruit has all of the nutrients your child needs, the Dietary Guidelines encourage you to offer a variety of them, and here's how.

- Offer your child a different type of vegetable and fruit each day. Let him serve himself, and if he doesn't care for it, he doesn't need to eat the rest. Just remember that research shows it can take up to eight to ten tries before your child actually will even taste a new food.
- Remember that while fresh produce is nutritious, so are frozen and canned vegetables and fruits. To get the biggest nutritional bang for your buck, select canned veggies without added salt, and canned or frozen fruits that are packed in natural juice.
- Sneak veggies and fruits into foods that your child enjoys. For example, toss red and green bell peppers into pasta sauce, or add raisins or shredded carrots in salads.

Somewhere over the Rainbow

Are you looking for a new way to encourage your grade-schooler to eat his veggies? Well, then, color your child's plate with a rainbow of vegetables and fruits. That way you can be sure that he's getting his five-a-day dose, along with a variety of vitamins, minerals, and disease-fighting phytonutrients.

Red	*tomatoes, watermelon, pink grapefruit*

A red color indicates the presence of *lycopene*, a phytonutrient that may help prevent cancer. While most phytonutrients are abundant in raw food, cooking concentrates lycopene. So that's good news for pizza lovers, because the sauce is loaded with lycopene. And go ahead and let your child put a small amount of ketchup on his foods because it's chock-full of lycopene too.

Orange	*pumpkins, carrots, yams, cantaloupe, oranges*

These brightly tinted vegetables and fruits contain *beta-carotene*. Carotenes are antioxidants that are being studied for their role in the prevention of cancer and heart disease.

Yellow	*squash, bell peppers, lemon peel*

When a yellow color is present, it's a signal that carotenes are in attendance. And citrus fruits, like lemons and grapefruits, contain *limonene*, which also may help prevent certain types of disease such as breast cancer.

Green	*broccoli, brussels sprouts, peas, artichokes*

Green produce contains another potentially powerful cancer fighter called *polyphenols*. Studies look promising that polyphenols may ward off cancers of the skin, esophagus, and prostate. Leafy, dark green vegetables, such as bok choy, kale, and spinach, also contain carotenes, just like orange and yellow produce.

Blue/Purple	*raisins, purple onions, eggplant, plums, dark-skinned grapes, blueberries*

(continued)

Yes, there really are naturally blue foods. And many of them contain *flavonoids, polyphenols,* or *ellagic acid,* which play a role in preventing heart disease and cancer.

White   *onions, garlic, leeks*

These pale produce contain hefty doses of *ally sulfides* and are associated with lowering cholesterol, blood pressure, and the risk of cancer.

Keep Foods Safe to Eat. Not only should the foods your child eats be healthy, but they also need to be safe for him to eat. That's why one of the Dietary Guidelines addresses food safety. It's not necessary to buy organic foods for your child (see chapter 10), because the food supply in this country is the safest in the world and regulated very closely by several government agencies including the Food and Drug Administration and the United States Department of Agriculture. And although you may find this hard to believe, the majority of food-related illnesses happen in the home, and not in the supermarket (see Chapter 8). Here are a few pointers on how to keep your grade-schooler safe at the plate.

- Encourage your child to wash his hands often. Proper hand washing may eliminate nearly half of all cases of food-borne illness and significantly reduce the spread of the common cold and flu.
- Keep raw meats and ready-to-eat foods (such as fruits or salads) separate from one another. Be careful with cutting boards. When juices from raw meats or germs from unclean objects accidentally touch cooked or ready-to-eat foods, cross-contamination can occur and cause a food-borne illness.

- Keep hot foods hot and cold foods cold. Foods from a meal should not be left out of a refrigerator or cooler for more than two hours. In hot weather (80 degrees F or above) this time is reduced to one hour. This will help slow the growth of bacteria and prevent food-borne illness.

C = Choose Sensibly

Choose a Diet That Is Low in Saturated Fat and Cholesterol and Moderate in Total Fat. Kids in this country are not only getting too fat but they're also eating too much of it. The particular culprit is saturated fat, which raises blood cholesterol levels. And studies have found that high blood cholesterol increases the risk of heart disease, the leading cause of death for adults in the United States today. To help prevent this insidious disease, which often begins early in life, the Dietary Guidelines recommend that after the age of two, everyone begin eating a diet that's lower in fat, saturated fat, and cholesterol. To help you come to "terms" with the different types of fat, here's a few basics.

- *Saturated Fats.* Foods that are high in saturated fats tend to raise blood cholesterol. These foods include high-fat dairy products (like cheese, whole milk, cream, butter, and regular ice cream), fatty fresh and processed meats, the skin and fat of poultry, lard, palm oil, and coconut oil. Try to keep your child's intake of these types of food low.
- *Unsaturated Fats.* Unsaturated fats do not raise blood cholesterol and are a better choice of fat than saturated fats. Unsaturated fats occur in vegetable oils, most nuts, olives, avocados, and fatty fish like salmon. Unsaturated oils include both monounsaturated fats and polyunsaturated fats. Olive, canola, sunflower, and peanut oils are some of the oils high in monounsaturated fats. Vegetable oils, such as soybean oil, corn oil, and cottonseed oil, and many kinds of nuts contain polyunsaturated fats. Some fish, such as salmon, tuna, and

mackerel, contain omega-3 fatty acids, which are being studied to determine if they offer protection against heart disease. Use moderate amounts of foods high in unsaturated fats, taking care to avoid excessive calories.

- *Trans-Fatty Acids.* Foods that are high in trans-fatty acids tend to raise blood cholesterol. These foods include those high in partially hydrogenated vegetable oils, such as many hard margarines and shortenings. Foods with a high amount of these ingredients include some commercially fried foods and some baked goods.

- *Dietary Cholesterol.* Foods that are high in cholesterol also tend to raise blood cholesterol. These foods include liver and other organ meats, egg yolks, and dairy fats, such as whole milk and cheese.

Choose Beverages and Foods to Moderate Your Intake of Sugars. Sugar—how sweet it is, but not necessarily when it comes to your child's health! Technically speaking, sugars are carbohydrates, just like starches, which fuel your child throughout the day with calories that help her grow. Sugar can occur naturally in foods like milk, fruits, some vegetables, breads, cereals, and grains, or it can be added to foods in processing or preparation. While your child's body can't tell the difference between naturally occurring or added sugars (because they're identical chemically), foods with added sugars, like soda, cakes, cookies, pies, fruit drinks, and candy, often provide too many calories and little or no nutrients.

Besides providing energy, sugar adds to the enjoyment of eating and to the flavor of foods. It also plays an important role in food preparation. But for all of its benefits, sugar still has a downside. While sugar will not cause your child to be hyperactive (as is commonly believed), studies have found that it can increase her risk of tooth decay. Also, foods that are high in added sugar are often high in calories and may cause your child to gain weight (see Chapter 10).

So how much sugar should your child have on a daily basis? The

Dietary Guidelines recommend that sugary foods and beverages be consumed in moderation. Make sure that your child eats foods from each of the five main foods groups *before* selecting foods from the fats, oils, and sweets category. In other words, kids should fill up on

---

What's Better for Your Child: Butter or Margarine?

The answer is margarine—but it has to be tub margarine. Butter contains a fairly large amount of saturated fat, which raises "bad" LDL cholesterol; margarine contains less saturated fat than butter, but if it's been hydrogenated (a process that makes the margarine harder), it contains trans-fatty acids, which can also raise LDL cholesterol. However, the softer and more spreadable the margarine, the fewer trans-fatty acids it contains.

In fact, a University of Texas study put forty-six families on two low-fat diet regimens, each lasting five weeks. One diet included butter; the other, tub margarine. When compared to the butter diet, the margarine-based diet lowered adults' LDL cholesterol (bad cholesterol) by 11 percent and children's by 9 percent. And just as important, the HDL cholesterol (good cholesterol) levels were not affected (sometimes HDLs drop on a low-fat diet, an undesirable side effect).

Here are a few tips to help you spread the wealth, and switch from butter to margarine.

- Always buy soft, tub-style margarine or check the front of the margarine package for trans-fatty acid–free claims.
- Read the label to make sure that the margarine has less than two grams of saturated fat.
- Scan the ingredient list for the words *hydrogenated* or *partially hydrogenated*, which means that the margarine contains trans-fatty acids. The lower down on the list they appear, the fewer trans-fatty acids there are.

nutritious foods before eating empty-calorie foods. Here are a few other pointers to help unsugar-coat your child's diet.

- Check out the Nutrition Facts Panel on food packages. You'll find the total amount of sugar listed there. Use this information to compare brands, and purchase the one with the least amount of sugar.
- Read the ingredient list to find out if sugar has been added. Keep in mind that sugar comes in many forms, so look for the following, which are other names for sugar: corn sweetener, corn syrup, honey, fruit juice concentrate, syrup, molasses, or any word ending in *ose*, like sucrose, fructose, or dextrose.
- Limit soft drinks. Soft drinks have replaced milk as the beverage of choice for many children. But a twelve-ounce can of soda contains a whopping *ten teaspoons* of added sugar and no nutrients. By comparison, an eight-ounce glass of low-fat milk contains just three teaspoons of natural sugar (lactose) and such beneficial nutrients as calcium, vitamin D, and protein.
- Offer reduced-sugar or sugar-free versions of foods. Many syrups, jams, cakes, pies, and cookies come in tasty reduced-sugar flavors. Or when baking, you can reduce the amount of sugar by one-fourth to one-third without affecting the taste.

Choose and Prepare Foods with Less Salt. In the body, sodium, which you get mainly from salt, plays a key role in regulating fluids and elevating blood pressure. Studies have found that people who eat a high-sodium diet are more likely to have high blood pressure. So if you can encourage your child to eat a diet with less salt, you may be able to ward off this future health problem. But this is often easier said than done. While only a small amount of sodium occurs naturally in foods, the majority of salt your child eats comes from foods that have been processed, like prepackaged cereals, chips, and luncheon meats, or what he adds to his food at the table.

How much salt should your child eat each day? The Nutrition

Facts Label on food packages lists a Daily Value of 2,400 milligrams or about one teaspoon of salt a day. Here are a few ways you can help your child shake the salt habit.

- Prepare foods with less, and eventually no salt. Your child's taste for salt will gradually decrease over time, so let him add a small amount at the table, and gradually cut back so that he learns to enjoy the natural flavor of foods.
- Look for processed foods that sport a "salt-free," "low-sodium," or "reduced-sodium" label. Also, use the Nutrition Facts Label to help you select the brand with the least amount of sodium (see Chapter 8).
- Use herbs and spices to flavor foods without adding salt. For starters, try adding fresh dill to steamed rice, curry powder to tuna salad, and basil to sliced tomatoes.

If You Drink Alcoholic Beverages, Do So in Moderation. This Dietary Guideline is obviously intended for adults. However, some children are drinking at very early ages, even during the grade school years. It's important to talk with your child about responsible drinking behaviors and the laws surrounding alcohol. Also, if you drink alcohol, make sure you are a good role model for your child. Never drink and drive.

EXTRA-CREDIT ASSIGNMENT

Rate Your Kid's Plate

Is your child a healthy eater? Find out by answering these questions about your child's daily food habits. Better yet, let your child take the quiz, and then compare your answers. Here's how to find out your score: For each question, if your answer is *always*, give yourself 5 points; *most of the time*, give yourself 3 points; and *sometimes*, give yourself 1 point. Then add up all your points for your total score.

Questions

1. Is your child an adventurous eater, and does he enjoy trying new foods?
2. Does your child eat at least six servings from the bread, cereal, rice, and pasta group of the Food Guide Pyramid each day?
3. Does your child eat at least three servings from the vegetable group each day?
4. Does your child eat at least two servings from the fruit group each day?
5. Does your child eat at least three servings from the milk, yogurt, and cheese group each day?
6. Does your child eat at least two servings from the meat, poultry, fish, dry beans, eggs, and nuts group each day?
7. Does your child drink soda and/or eat candy and sugary foods in moderation?
8. Does your child enjoy eating fiber-rich foods, such as whole-grain breads and cereals, fruits, and vegetables?
9. Does your child drink skim or 1-percent milk and eat low-fat dairy products?

(continued)

Rate Your Kid's Plate (continued)

10. Does your child eat chicken, turkey, fish, and lean cuts of meat that are baked, broiled, or grilled—not fried?
11. Does your child snack on low or reduced-fat foods, such as pretzels, low-fat cookies, and crackers?
12. Is your child physically active? Does she shoot hoops, ride a bike, jump rope, etc., for at least sixty minutes a day?

Rating Scale

45–60 points: Your child's a lean, keen eating machine. Keep up the good work.

30–44 points: Your child's engine could use some fine-tuning. Check out "How to Boost Your Child's Score."

Fewer than 30 points: Your child's running on empty. Don't give up, because it's not too late to help him develop good eating habits. Check out "How to Boost Your Child's Score," and ask your pediatrician or a registered dietitian to help you create a workable plan for your child.

How to Boost Your Child's Score

While there are no right or wrong answers, each question addresses important eating behaviors.

Question 1: Serve Up Variety. Variety plays a key role in your child's diet. A growing child requires more than 40 different nutrients, and no single food can provide them all. Go back and review Exploring the Pyramids earlier in this chapter.

Questions 2 through 6: Focus on the Food Guide Pyramid. The Food Guide Pyramid can help you make sure your child's diet is nutritionally balanced. Go back and review Exploring the Pyramids, earlier in this chapter.

(continued)

Rate Your Kid's Plate (continued)

Question 7: Slow Down on the Sweets. All foods—even soda and candy—can fit into a healthy diet when eaten in limited quantities. Go back and review the Dietary Guideline: *Choose beverages and foods to moderate your sugar intake*, earlier in this chapter.

Question 8: Fill Up on Fiber. Children, like adults, need fiber to help them reduce their risk of future health problems, such as cancer and heart disease. Go back and review the Dietary Guideline: *Choose a variety of grains, especially whole grains*, earlier in this chapter.

Questions 9 through 11: Forgo a Little Fat. Fat is an essential nutrient that provides children with energy for growth and development, and it enables the body to absorb the fat-soluble vitamins A, D, E, and K. But after your child's second birthday, it's important to start trimming the fat from her diet to help ward off future heart and weight problems. Go back and review the Dietary Guideline: *Choose a diet that is low in saturated fat and cholesterol and moderate in total fat*, earlier in this chapter.

Question 12: Shake It Up, Baby. Lack of physical activity has become an epidemic in our country. Kids need to combine healthy eating with fun, daily physical activity like bike riding, jumping rope, or even walking the dog. Go back and review the Dietary Guideline: *Be physically active each day*, earlier in this chapter.

CHAPTER 3

Breakfast for Brain Power

◆ ◆ ◆

I don't have time for breakfast, I've gotta wash my hair.
—JENNY, SIXTH GRADE

I'm just not hungry in the morning.
—KYLE, SECOND GRADE

I don't like breakfast foods.
—TIMMY, FIFTH GRADE

Top Three Breakfast Mistakes Parents Make:

1. Let kids skip breakfast.
2. Provide skimpy or boring breakfasts.
3. Don't eat breakfast themselves.

There are many reasons why one out of every eight school-age children starts the day without eating breakfast. But if your child has an excuse (even a good one!), don't buy it; breakfast, arguably the most important meal of the day, is too crucial to miss. Read on, and find out how you can wake up your child's

49

appetite and make this early morning meal a real favorite. In this chapter you'll:

- find out how breakfast and learning go hand in hand;
- design a meal that meets with our Five-Star Breakfast Criteria and earns your child's approval;
- select a strategy you can use to help your grade-schooler break the breakfast-skipping habit.

BREAKFAST: AN EYE-OPENING EXPERIENCE

Because both of us are working mothers, with a houseful of grade-schoolers, we understand how hectic things can get in the morning and why your child may choose to snooze rather than eat breakfast. But sound the alarm. Kids who take a pass on breakfast are missing out on more than just a tasty meal. Breakfast skippers tend to perform poorly and behave inappropriately in school and may be at risk for future health problems like obesity and heart disease. And now we have more than thirty years of breakfast research to back this up. Here are some of the key reasons why you should jump-start your child's day with breakfast.

Eating Breakfast Can Help Your Child . . .

boost test scores. Kids who eat breakfast are more alert and perform better on school tests than kids who skip the morning meal. They are also more creative and energetic. Hunger, even short-term hunger that your child may experience if she misses breakfast, can decrease her attention span and concentration abilities. This can be particularly hard on younger grade-schoolers because basic subjects like writing and arithmetic are often taught first thing in the morning. The bottom line: Hungry kids just can't do their best work.

improve school attendance. Children who eat breakfast are absent fewer days and spend less time in the school nurse's office complaining of tummy aches and more time in the classroom learning. And as ironic as it might sound, kids who skip breakfast because they claim they don't have enough time are tardy coming to class more often than kids who take the time to eat breakfast.

behave better. Kids who regularly eat a morning meal have a better attitude toward school and more energy by late morning. Breakfast skippers tend to feel tired, irritable, or restless in the morning and have problems with anxiety and aggression.

stay energized. Children who eat breakfast tend to have more strength and endurance than kids who don't. Eating breakfast provides them with the calories they need, which can bolster their stamina and keep them active throughout the day.

eat a more nutritious diet. Kids' overall nutrition improves when they eat breakfast. That's because they have a much better chance of meeting their daily requirements from the Food Guide Pyramid which supplies key nutrients (see Chapter 2). On average, a breakfast eater's diet tends to contain more fiber, vitamins, and minerals—especially calcium, vitamin C, and folic acid. Also, children who skip breakfast typically do not make up for the missed nutrients at other meals.

keep weight under control. Sitting down to a morning meal establishes a regular eating pattern (a rapidly disappearing practice in many families) that's key to weight control throughout life. Kids who eat meals at set times are better able to regulate their appetite and are less likely to overeat and snack on fatty, sugary foods.

lower blood cholesterol. Although the jury is still out, research has shown that kids who eat breakfast *tend* to have lower blood cholesterol levels than kids who say no to a morning meal. Having high blood cholesterol places a child at risk for future health problems such as heart disease.

BREAKFAST BASICS FOR BUSY FAMILIES

The word *breakfast* literally means "breaking the fast." After a full night's sleep, your child's body has gone eight to ten hours without taking in any sustenance. It needs to replenish its "fuel source" by eating nutritious foods. The kinds of foods that your child eats for breakfast can make a big difference in her energy level.

Fill Up with the Right Mix of Fuel

If your child eats breakfast but feels tired and hungry after only a few hours, chances are she's not getting the right mix of fuel or energy from the foods she's consuming. A breakfast that consists primarily of sugary foods like fruit, fruit juice, candy, or soda, will provide a quick burst of energy. Blood sugar levels will surge, but after about one hour they'll plummet, leaving your child with that hungry feeling again.

Eating a balanced breakfast that consists of carbohydrates, protein, and modest amounts of fat will help get your child going—and keep her going—all morning long. That's because foods with these nutrients supply the right mix of energy and provide it in a sustained manner over time. Eating this combination of fuels also helps to maintain blood sugar levels and ward off hunger until the lunch bell rings (see figure next page).

WHAT DOES A BALANCED BREAKFAST LOOK LIKE?

To help you identify a balanced breakfast so you can offer it to your child, we've put together our Five-Star Breakfast Criteria. In order for a breakfast to be considered "balanced," it must earn a rating of five stars. We encourage you to use these guidelines to plan and then evaluate your child's breakfast. Better yet, teach your grade-schooler how to use the criteria himself to rate his own breakfast.

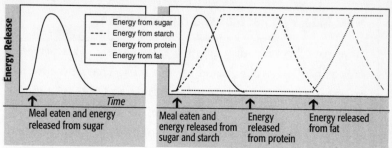

Sugary foods, such as fruit, fruit juice, candy, or soda pop, eaten in place of a meal cause a quick rise in blood sugar and energy. About an hour later blood sugar and energy decline rapidly, bringing on symptoms of hunger.

Balanced breakfast containing sugar, starch, protein, and fat (like a typical school breakfast containing fruit or juice, toast or cereal and 2 percent of whole milk) gives a sustained release of energy in children, delaying symptoms of hunger for several hours.

The American Dietetic Association's Complete Food and Nutrition Guide

Five-Star Breakfast Criteria

A breakfast should earn one star for meeting each of the following five criteria. (See Chapter 2 for more detailed information about each of them.)

- ★ The breakfast provides at least one selection from three or more different food groups.
- ★ It contains no more than one item from the nutritionally lacking fats, oils, and sweets category.
- ★ It includes high-fiber foods, like whole-grain breads and cereals, fruits, vegetables, dry beans, nuts, and seeds.
- ★ Its fat content has been reduced.
- ★ Your child actually ate and enjoyed the breakfast—after all, a breakfast that's not eaten, no matter how balanced, isn't nourishing.

Milk: Moo-ving Fat Makes a Big Difference

Have you checked out your milk carton lately? Two percent milk is no longer considered low-fat milk. That's because in order for a food or beverage to be considered "low-fat" it must contain no more than three grams of fat per serving. While all types of milk are excellent sources of protein, carbohydrate, and calcium, moving the fat out makes a big difference in calories.

1 cup of:	has:
whole milk	150 calories; 8 grams of fat
2 percent milk or reduced-fat milk	120 calories; 5 grams of fat
1 percent or low-fat milk	100 calories; 2.5 grams of fat
skim or fat-free milk	80 calories; 0 grams of fat

Sample Five-Star Breakfast

Here's an example of a balanced breakfast that meets our five-star criteria. And it just so happens to be one of our kids' favorites.

Sample Breakfast Menu. 1 8-ounce carton of low-fat strawberry yogurt; 1 whole-grain cinnamon-swirl bagel; ¾ cup calcium-fortified orange juice

Nutrition Analysis. Let's review why this breakfast meets our criteria.

- It contains at least three food groups: low-fat yogurt = milk group, bagel = grain group, and orange juice = fruit group.
- There are no servings from the fats, oils, and sweets category.
- The whole-grain bagel is a high-fiber food.
- The fat content has been lowered by serving low-fat yogurt.
- The entire meal was eaten.

The Egg-ceptional Egg

Eggs have really gotten a bad rap. They're an excellent source of protein, which kids need to grow and to remain healthy. One large egg has six grams of protein, about half of which is found in the egg white. The egg yolk is where you'll find all of the dietary cholesterol. And, thanks to better measuring techniques, and chicken breeding and feeding practices, eggs have less cholesterol than was reported in the past. In fact, the newly revised American Heart Association (AHA) Guidelines recognize that egg yolks have less cholesterol, about 213 to 220 milligrams per yolk, compared to the previous value of 300 milligrams or more. And based on this new research, they no longer encourage people to limit their egg yolk consumption. Rather, the AHA continues to recommend that adults and children over the age of two limit their *total* dietary cholesterol intake to 300 milligrams or less per day, which means your child could potentially have up to one whole egg a day. Here are some thoughts on how to help keep your spirits sunny side up.

- Egg whites have no cholesterol. So if one egg doesn't seem like enough to satisfy your child's appetite, you can substitute two egg whites for one whole egg or purchase a carton of egg substitutes and scramble them.
- Eggs are quick and easy to prepare. They come naturally packaged in their own "single-serving" shell and take only minutes to cook. So it's easy to whip up a quick meal or snack for your child without a lot of waste.
- Eggs are a nutritional bargain. No other animal protein costs less than a carton of eggs. Serving egg-based dinners like quiche or souffle can help trim dollars off your food budget.

ANALYZE THIS: REAL-LIFE BREAKFAST MAKEOVERS

How do *real* kids' breakfasts stack up against our Five-Star Breakfast Criteria? To find out, we spent several mornings eating breakfast with some of our kids' friends and their families. Here's how some of their favorite morning meals fared.

How Sweet It Is Menu

> 2 chocolate-frosted doughnuts with vanilla cream filling
> 1 8-ounce fruit drink
> Rating: ★

Nutrition Analysis. Joseph, a sixth-grader, loves doughnuts with frosting because he likes something sweet to eat in the morning. But unfortunately, his breakfast contains only one food group (doughnuts = grain group), and several selections from the fats, oils, and sweets category (the fruit drink, frosting on the doughnuts, and vanilla cream filling). Also no attempts were made to increase the fiber or decrease the fat in Joseph's breakfast. The only reason the breakfast earned one star is because Joseph ate all of it.

How to Raise His Breakfast Grade. If your child, like Joseph, craves something sweet for breakfast, it's fine to offer doughnuts every once in a while. But keep in mind, they are loaded with fat and sugar. To satisfy your child's early morning sweet tooth, try offering whole-grain toaster waffles with reduced-sugar syrup. And on days when doughnuts are on your breakfast menu, add another food group by serving low-fat milk, and offer a slice of melon or some fresh berries for fiber.

The Breakfast-Skimper Menu

> 1 slice of white toast with
> 1 tablespoon peanut butter
> 1 cup water
> Rating: ★★

Nutrition Analysis. Mattie, a kindergartner, really doesn't have much of an appetite in the morning, and his mom says it's a struggle to get him to eat even this much. Lots of kids share Mattie's early morning, not-so-hungry syndrome. Mattie's breakfast consists of foods from two food groups (the toast = grain group, and the peanut butter = protein group). However, the peanut butter is a bit too skimpy to be considered a full serving (two tablespoons of peanut butter = one serving from the protein group). The good news is that Mattie has no selections from the fats, oils, and sweets category, and he *does* eat his breakfast. But unfortunately, his breakfast is low in fiber, and no attempts were made to reduce the fat content.

How to Raise His Breakfast Grade. To make the most of his small appetite, Mattie needs to pack a nutritional punch into everything he eats. For starters, he should switch to whole-grain toast to boost fiber and use reduced-fat peanut butter, but increase the portion size to two tablespoons. Also, a glass of low-fat milk or calcium-fortified orange juice would offer more nutrients than the glass of water. He may want to eat half of his toast at home and take the other half to eat on the bus or as a snack at school if his teacher will allow it.

The Egg Head Menu

2 scrambled eggs
2 strips of bacon
½ bagel with 1 teaspoon margarine
1 cup of 2 percent milk
Rating: ★★★

Nutrition Analysis. Kimberly, a third-grader, usually only eats this breakfast on the weekend because her mom believes that eggs have a lot of cholesterol. Kimberly's breakfast contains three food groups (the eggs = protein group, the bagel = grain group, and the 2 percent milk = dairy group). Although Kimberly and her mom have made attempts to reduce fat by drinking 2 percent milk, the bacon and the margarine still contribute a hefty amount of it. And while Kimberly does eat all of her breakfast, it's lacking in fiber.

How to Raise Her Breakfast Grade. Kimberly's breakfast can easily be transformed to meet our Five-Star Breakfast Criteria. All she would need to do is eat a whole-grain bagel for a fiber boost, and switch to Canadian bacon, which is much lower in fat than regular bacon, and would therefore count as a meat group serving (bacon counts as a serving from the fats, oils, and sweets category). Also, spreading jam on her bagel instead of margarine would trim the fat even more, but if she prefers a buttery taste, she could use a reduced-fat margarine spread. Also, switching to lower-fat milk, like 1 percent or skim, would reduce her fat intake even more.

BREAKING THE BREAKFAST-SKIPPING BARRIERS

As parents you understand why eating breakfast is important, but what do your kids think? A national survey of one thousand children between the ages of nine and twelve, conducted for Post cereal, revealed that kids do understand that eating breakfast is *great* for them. In fact, the survey said . . .

- 90 percent acknowledged that breakfast helps them learn
- 87 percent thought that they pay attention better after eating breakfast
- 85 percent felt "more awake" and "smarter" at school after they had eaten a morning meal

Yet despite this awareness, the survey indicated that nearly 40 percent of the participants were not eating breakfast at least once a week—and as many as 7 percent were missing breakfast between five and seven times each week.

If you have a breakfast skipper in your household, here are some strategies that you and your child can employ to make sure that he starts the day with a healthy meal.

Beating the Morning Rush Hour

Do you play "beat the clock" every morning? If so, these fast-breaking tips can offer a speedy start to your day.

- *Save breakfast prep time.* Set out bowls, utensils, and any non-perishable food, such as cereal sans the milk, the night before.
- *Sound the alarm early.* Try getting your child up ten minutes earlier so that he has time for breakfast.
- *Pack lunches and plan wardrobes in advance.* Make lunches and refrigerate them the night before, and have your child lay out her school clothes so they're ready in the morning.
- *Establish a breakfast routine.* Give each family member a breakfast responsibility—one person prepares breakfast, the other cleans up.
- *Just say no to TV and computers.* Watching cartoons and checking e-mail eats up valuable time in the morning and takes time away from eating breakfast.
- *Keep breakfast simple.* Save those stacks of pancakes smothered in maple syrup and bacon and eggs for weekends. Serve quick breakfast items, like instant oatmeal with raisins and a glass of milk, during the school week.
- *Encourage your child to help you plan a breakfast menu each week.* The planning can be done anywhere, even in the car while you're driving to soccer practice. Ask your child what he would like to eat for breakfast, and make sure that you keep those items on hand.
- *Swing by the drive-through window.* If you drive your child to school, pick up a quick breakfast at a fast-food restaurant or nearby coffee bar. These places offer several nutritious foods, like pancakes or egg sandwiches, that can help fuel your child for the morning.

Breakfast Quick Picks

When you're on the go and fast food is your only option, order these light and lean breakfasts to help your grade-schooler be bright and keen. Each breakfast meets our Five-Star Breakfast Criteria. You'll find them at most fast-food restaurants, coffee shops, or convenience stores.

Hurry-Up Hot Cakes

pancakes (hold the butter, and go easy on the syrup)
yogurt and fruit cup
orange juice

Let's Get Crackin' Egg Sandwich

scrambled eggs
whole-grain bagel
low-fat milk

Get Movin' Muffins

reduced-fat bran muffin
banana (you may need to bring this from home)
low-fat milk

Waking Up a Groggy Tummy

Many kids complain that they just don't feel like eating when they get up. If this is true for your child, here are some things you can do.

- *Consider a progressive breakfast.* Have your child eat a piece of fruit and drink a glass of milk before he leaves the house. Then on the bus, he can eat an oatmeal muffin or a breakfast cereal bar.

- *Create a breakfast sandwich.* Pack a peanut butter-and-banana sandwich made from a whole-wheat bagel, or try a whole-grain pita pocket filled with ricotta cheese and apple slices sprinkled with cinnamon.
- *Eat breakfast at school.* Many schools now serve a variety of nutritious breakfasts for kids before school in the cafeteria.
- *Take a break from the ordinary, and try some not-so-traditional breakfast foods.* Pizza, leftover chicken, and grilled cheese are all perfectly acceptable foods to eat for breakfast. Remember, it's not *what* your child eats but *when* she eats it that makes it breakfast.
- *Be a role model and eat breakfast.* If your child sees you making the time to eat a nourishing meal, she is more than likely to follow your good example.

BREAKFAST IS SERVED!

One of the best ways to ensure that your child eats breakfast is to always have plenty of foods on hand. Stock your pantry and freezer with nutritious items that can easily be assembled into a quick and tasty breakfast. Keep a note pad handy so that you can jot down items as you run out of them and replace them on your next trip to the grocery store. Teach your breakfast inventory system to your older grade-schooler so that he can help keep the shopping list updated.

How to Stock a Breakfast Bar

Here are some foods you can use to set up a breakfast bar in your very own kitchen. Put some of these foods in your refrigerator:

Grain Group: tortillas
Vegetable Group: green onions, red or green bell peppers, salsa, tomato juice, premade hash brown potatoes
Fruit Group: orange juice (regular and calcium-fortified); fresh fruit like apples, pears, melons, and berries

Smart Choice: The School Breakfast Program

Does your child have no time for breakfast at home? Check with your school to see if it offers a breakfast program. The School Breakfast Program (SBP) is a federally assisted meal program that operates in more than 70,000 schools around the country. It provides nutritionally balanced meals to 7 million children each school day. And the breakfasts are available free, or at a reduced cost, to students meeting certain income eligibility requirements. The program was established under the Child Nutrition Act of 1966 to ensure that all children have access to a healthy breakfast at school and to promote learning readiness and healthy eating behaviors. Over the past ten years, the number of kids eating breakfast at school has nearly doubled. And according to studies conducted by the American School Food Service Association, breakfasts offered by the SBP tend to be more nutritious than those served at home. Here are a few ways to get the most out of the SBP.

- Talk with your principal and school board, and discuss whether your school-lunch program can be expanded to include breakfast too.
- Find out if your child is eligible for reduced-cost or free breakfasts by visiting www.fns.usda.gov/cnd/Breakfast. Or check with your school food-service manager.
- If your school offers a breakfast plan, ask the cafeteria personnel for a menu in advance. That way you can go over meal options with your child.

Dairy Group: low-fat milk; low-fat yogurt; shredded, string, and sliced cheese; reduced-fat ricotta cheese; and chocolate milk
Protein Group: eggs, egg substitutes, hard-boiled eggs, Canadian bacon, and lox.

Stock your freezer with these foods and thaw them when you need them:

Grain Group: whole-wheat bread, whole-grain waffles and pancakes, pita bread, English muffins, bran muffins, bagels, and whole-grain buns
Vegetable Group: frozen vegetables
Fruit Group: frozen 100 percent fruit juice concentrate like orange or pineapple; frozen fruit such as strawberries and blueberries
Protein Group: Canadian bacon, lean ham, and egg substitutes

Make sure your pantry is filled with these foods:

Grain Group: ready-to-eat cereal, quick-cooking oatmeal, wheat germ, granola, breakfast bars
Vegetable Group: canned vegetables, such as tomatoes, green peas, and corn
Fruit Group: applesauce; fruit canned in natural juice like pineapple and peaches; dried fruit like raisins and cranberries; bananas
Protein Group: reduced-fat nut butters like peanut butter or almond butter, refried beans, nuts, and seeds

One-Minute Breakfast Ideas

When your whole family is in a hurry, and you want to serve a fast breakfast, try offering your child one of these grab-and-go meals. All of them meet our 5-Star Breakfast Criteria. Although kids of all ages will enjoy eating these breakfasts, any meal with a (★) may be more appealing to an older grade-schooler.

You Go, Cereal! Eat half a carton of low-fat yogurt then mix in a ready-to-eat whole-grain cereal, and serve with a glass of calcium-fortified orange juice.

Shake It Up, Baby★ Whir low-fat milk, frozen strawberries, and a banana in a blender for thirty seconds. Slurp it down with a bran muffin.

Waz Up Waffles★ Pop frozen whole-grain waffles into the toaster, and top with vanilla low-fat yogurt and fresh berries.

Banana Dogs Spread reduced-fat peanut butter in a hot dog bun; plop in a banana, and sprinkle with raisins.

Pita Pockets★ Stuff a whole-grain pita pocket with ricotta cheese and Granny Smith apple slices; add a dash of cinnamon.

Hula-Hula Hot Cakes Microwave frozen pancakes, then top them with pineapple rings and a dab of reduced-sugar syrup; wash everything down with a glass of low-fat chocolate milk.

Mexican Toasted Cheese★ Sprinkle grated Monterey Jack cheese over a corn tortilla; fold in half, and microwave for twenty seconds. Top with salsa.

Breakfast Parfait Layer a parfait cup with low-fat yogurt, berries, and granola.

Fruit and Nut Oatmeal★ Add dried cranberries and almonds to quick-cooking oatmeal, and microwave for sixty seconds.

In-the-Bag Breakfast In a zipper-type plastic bag, mix together ready-to-eat cereal, dried fruits such as raisins or chopped dates, and nuts like peanuts or chopped pecans.

Weekend Specials

For those rare lazy mornings when everyone has an opportunity to catch a few extra winks, go ahead and try some of our families' favorite brunch mainstays.

◆ ◆ ◆

Overnight French Toast

makes 6 servings

nonstick vegetable spray
8 thick slices of whole-wheat bread
8 large eggs
3 cups skim milk
1 tablespoon vanilla extract
1 teaspoon cinnamon
reduced-sugar maple syrup

Coat a 9" × 13" baking pan with nonstick spray. Place the bread completely over the bottom of the pan. Whisk together the eggs, milk, vanilla, and cinnamon in a large bowl. Pour this mixture over the bread. Cover with aluminum foil, and refrigerate overnight.

Preheat oven to 350 degrees F. Remove the foil, and bake uncovered about 40 to 50 minutes, until the bread is puffed and golden brown. Let stand five minutes before serving with syrup.

Tip: Serve the French toast with fresh berries and a glass of low-fat milk.

◆ ◆ ◆

Scrambled Egg Pizza

makes 8 servings

1 16-ounce loaf frozen whole-wheat bread dough, thawed
6 eggs
½ cup skim milk
nonstick vegetable spray

½ cup pizza sauce
¾ cup part-skim mozzarella cheese, shredded
4 strips turkey bacon, cooked and crumbled

On a lightly floured surface, roll the dough into a 13-inch circle, then put it on a greased 13-inch pizza pan. Build up the edges to make a crust, then prick the dough generously with a fork. Bake at 375 degrees F for 15 minutes or until light brown.

While the crust is baking, beat the eggs and milk together in a large bowl. Coat a skillet with nonstick spray, and heat until a drop of water sizzles Pour in the egg mixture, and scramble.

Spread the sauce over the baked crust, and sprinkle with half of the cheese. Top with the scrambled eggs and remaining cheese, and toss the bacon over the top. Bake five more minutes or until the cheese melts.

Note: Serve the pizza with a glass of calcium-fortified orange juice.

◆ ◆ ◆

EXTRA-CREDIT ASSIGNMENT

The Breakfast Club

Planning a five-star breakfast is as easy as one-two-three food groups! To give you a head start on your breakfast planning, add a third food group to the breakfast items already listed in the chart on page 67. Then compare your breakfast to the Five-Star-Breakfast Criteria covered earlier in this chapter. After you've aced the test, go ahead and let your child see what he can plan.

Five-Star Breakfast Criteria

DAY OF THE WEEK	FOOD GROUP	FOOD GROUP	FOOD GROUP
Monday		1 cup oatmeal (grain group)	1 cup low-fat milk (dairy group)
Tuesday		2 hard-boiled eggs (protein group)	¾ cup orange juice (fruit group)
Wednesday		½ cup strawberries (fruit group)	1 cup low-fat milk (dairy group)
Thursday		½ whole-grain bagel (grain group)	⅔ cup tomato juice (vegetable group)
Friday		1 ounce raisin bran cereal (grain group)	1 cup low-fat milk (dairy group)
Saturday		1 pancake (grain group)	½ cup blueberries (fruit group)
Sunday		1 link reduced-fat sausage (protein group)	1 cup low-fat milk (dairy group)

CHAPTER 4

Lunch Lessons

◆ ◆ ◆

I never eat all *of my lunch because my mom*
gives me too much.
—KRISTIN, FIRST GRADE

I always trade my white milk to Brendan for his chocolate milk.
—J.J., FIFTH GRADE

I don't have enough time to eat all of my lunch,
so I only eat the dessert.
—SAM, THIRD GRADE

Top Three Lunch Mistakes Parents Make:

1. Assume their kids eat all of their lunch.
2. Pack too much food.
3. Believe school hot lunch is not nutritious.

Do you know what your child ate for lunch today at school? If you answered yes because you packed her lunch or selected it from the school menu, chances are you might be wrong. In fact, on any given day, approximately one out of every four students trades her lunch or tosses it into the trash. This chapter is loaded with sure-bet information to help you improve the odds that your child will eat—and enjoy—her lunch. In this chapter you will:

- discover the benefits to both brown-bagging and buying your child's meal at school;
- design a meal that meets our Five-Star Lunch Criteria and that your child wouldn't dream of trading;
- learn several tips for packing the *coolest* lunch box and picking the *hottest* school lunch.

LET'S DO LUNCH!

Eating a nutritious, well-balanced lunch during the school day is important. It helps your child concentrate better in the classroom and improve his ability to learn. A good lunch can also supply some of the energy your child needs to participate in after-school sports and activities. But is it better for your child to bring a lunch from home or buy it at school? The answer to this age-old question is arguable, but it really depends on what *you* send, because both options have their benefits. Here are a few things you'll want to consider when deciding whether to bag or to buy.

With brown-bagging, you can . . .

- *control the types of food provided.* This is particularly helpful if your child has a food intolerance or allergy.
- *eliminate waste.* Because you're in charge of portion sizes, you can send smaller or larger amounts of foods.
- *aim to please.* A homemade lunch enables you to cater to your child's individual likes and dislikes for various foods.

With the School-Lunch Program, you can . . .

- *beat the morning rush hour.* Buying lunch helps you avoid early morning hassles and delays about what to pack for lunch.
- *offer greater variety.* A hot lunch from the school cafeteria often provides your child with more meal options, including foods that are difficult to pack, like tacos and steamed veggies.
- *potentially save money.* Buying a lunch at school is typically more cost-effective than bringing a lunch from home. And often, school lunches are available at a reduced fee or free of charge to students who meet certain eligibility criteria.

School Lunch vs. Lunches Brought from Home: The Great Nutrition Debate

The results are in, and school lunches win! A recent study conducted at the University of Eastern Michigan evaluated more than 560 lunches of second-, third-, and fourth-grade students and concluded that the school lunches were generally lower in fat, provided more nutrients, and offered more food variety than the lunches brought from home. How can that be? Thanks to the School Meals Initiative for Healthy Children, a federal program initiated in 1996, all schools participating in the National School Lunch Program (NSLP) must now provide lunches that supply children with one-third of their daily requirements for calories and nutrients, *and* comply with the United States Department of Agriculture's (USDA) Dietary Guidelines for Americans (see Chapter 2).

In order to meet these guidelines, schools must:

- add more vegetables, fruits, and whole grains to their menus;
- create more balanced meals by selecting foods from each of the five food groups;
- reduce fat content in lunches by using less beef, offering vegetarian entrees, and serving fewer fried foods;
- introduce more ethnic entrees to increase variety.

According to the latest USDA evaluation of the NSLP, schools are indeed supplying kids with healthier meals. In 1999, 82 percent of the grade schools participating in the NSLP were offering lunches that were lower in fat compared to just 34 percent in the 1991–92 school year. In addition, nearly all school lunch menus included at least two choices of milk and roughly two-thirds of all lunch menus offered more than the required two fruit and vegetable choices. If your child would like to buy her lunch at school, consider the following:

- Ask your principal if your school participates in the NSLP. If it doesn't, then there's no guarantee that the lunches served are meeting the Dietary Guidelines.
- If your school does participate in the NSLP, check with the principal or cafeteria manager to see if your child is eligible for lunches at a reduced cost or free of charge.
- Find out if you can obtain copies of the school lunch menus in advance. Then go over the menus with your child before she makes her selections at school.

THE ANATOMY OF A HEALTHY LUNCH

Since all schools do not participate in the NSLP, and because some children simply prefer to bring their own, it's important that you, and your child, know how to pack a lunch with a nutritional punch. To help everyone with their packing, we've put together our Five-Star Lunch Criteria. For a lunch to be considered balanced, it must earn a rating of five stars. We encourage you and your child to use these guidelines to first plan the lunch menu and then to evaluate your progress.

Five-Star Lunch Criteria

A lunch should receive one star for meeting each of the following five criteria. (See Chapter 2 for more detailed information about each of them.)

★ The lunch provides at least one selection from each of the five food groups.

★ It contains no more than one item from the nutritionally lacking fats, oils, and sweets category.

★ It includes high-fiber foods like whole-grain breads and cereals, vegetables, fruits, dry beans, nuts, and seeds.

★ Its fat content has been reduced.

★ Your child actually ate and enjoyed the lunch—after all, a lunch that ends up in the trash, or somebody else's tummy, won't nourish your child.

Sample Five-Star Lunch

Here's an example of a balanced lunch that meets our criteria and that our kids enjoy eating at school.

Sample Lunch Menu. Sandwich: two ounces of turkey, one ounce of reduced-fat Swiss cheese on two slices of whole-wheat bread with a teaspoon of mayonnaise; half cup of baby carrots; one Granny Smith apple; one eight-ounce carton of low-fat milk

Nutrition Analysis. Let's review why this lunch meets our criteria.

It contains all five food groups: whole-grain bread = grain group, baby carrots = vegetable group, Granny Smith apple = fruit group, reduced-fat Swiss cheese and low-fat milk = dairy group, and turkey = protein group.

There is only one serving from the fats, oils, and sweets category, and that's the mayonnaise.

The whole-grain bread, baby carrots, and apple all provide fiber.

The fat content of the lunch has been lowered by choosing turkey over high-fat luncheon meats, using reduced-fat Swiss cheese, and selecting low-fat milk.

The entire meal was eaten.

CAN THIS LUNCH BE SAVED?

Now that we've established some of the criteria for a healthy, well-balanced lunch, let's look at what we found in the "real world." While sleuthing through our children's school lunchrooms, we spied everything from kids discarding the majority of their lunch to those who were willing to trade an entire meal for one large cookie. Here are some of our observations—and, of course, the names have been changed to protect the innocent!

The Snacker

    25 mini cheese-sandwich crackers
    1 cup corn chips
    20 mini chocolate chip cookies
    10 bite-size chocolate bars
    1 12-ounce can orange soda
    Rating: ★

The lunch that Patrick chose is typical of kids who prefer to "graze," or eat smaller meals—often snack foods—throughout the day. The first-grader says he doesn't really care for sandwiches. His mom says he's finicky and doesn't eat much meat. Three days a week, Patrick picks out foods for lunch; the other two days Mom makes the selection. This meal was one of Patrick's choices.

Nutrition Analysis. Mom's right in her approach to handling a picky eater—forcing kids to eat foods they don't like may lead to eating problems later in life (see Chapter 10). In fact, there's nothing wrong with "grazing," but it is important to offer smaller amounts of nutrient-rich foods. Patrick's lunch lacks selections from the vegetable, fruit, milk, and meat groups. It contains soda and candy, which count as choices from the fats, oil, and sweets category. And all of his grain-group selections, for instance the cheese crackers, corn chips, and cookies, are low in fiber and high in fat. The portions are a bit hefty, too. But because Patrick ate his entire lunch, it earned a one-star rating.

How to Raise His Lunch Grade. Instead of packing soda, which contains about ten teaspoons of sugar and no nutrients, Patrick's mom could give him 100 percent fruit juice. In lieu of a sandwich, which Patrick admits he doesn't like, his mom could send a couple of hard-boiled eggs and a carton of low-fat yogurt. To boost the fiber content of his lunch, yet satisfy his craving for sweet and salty foods, she could pack a trail mix of chopped nuts, raisins, whole-grain cereal, sunflower seeds, with a few chocolate chips tossed inside.

The Castaway

1 prepackaged deli lunch, which included:
2 soft-shell tacos with Cajun meat sauce
1 small can of fruit cocktail
1 carton of low-fat milk
Rating: ★★

Megan, who's in second grade, loves Mexican food, but she's not crazy about the meat sauce that came with the tacos. In fact, she ate one taco with nothing on it and the fruit cocktail and drank all of her milk. Megan's father usually packs her lunch and typically includes only three items, such as a peanut butter and jelly sandwich, a handful of chips, and some fresh fruit. On days when they're really in a hurry, though, he relies on prepackaged meals.

Nutrition Analysis. Megan's lunch earned two stars because it contained low-fat milk and no items from the fats and sweets category. Unfortunately, while it included most of the food groups, the vegetable group was missing, it didn't provide much fiber, and the majority of her meal ended up being "cast away" in the trash, because she didn't like the meat sauce and had a difficult time opening each of the preportioned items.

How to Raise Her Lunch Grade. Like Megan's family, we're all pressed for time in the morning. So to beat the clock, you can pack your child's lunch the night before, and store it in the refrigerator. Also, keep prepackaged nutrient-rich foods on hand, such as whole-grain granola bars or raisins. If Megan really wants Mexican food for lunch, her dad could spread a can of fat-free refried beans on a corn tortilla, and top it with some grated reduced-fat cheddar cheese. He could pour some salsa into a small plastic container, and send along some celery sticks for dipping. He could also pack some fresh fruit for added fiber.

The Trader

Denise bought a school lunch that included:

> pasta with meat sauce
> garlic bread
> 1 banana
> 1 chocolate chip cookie
> 1 carton of low-fat milk
> (She traded everything except her milk and garlic bread for one
> large chocolate-frosted cookie.)
> Rating: ★★★★

Like most kids, fourth-grader Denise traded her lunch because she didn't like what was offered. Her mom says she lets Denise pick her own meals from the school menu, but the real problem is in her school, students are required to order a week's worth of meals at a time. Typically, Denise likes what's offered three out of the five days each week. On days that she doesn't like what's offered, Denise takes a sandwich, yogurt, or fruit. As for the trade, Denise has a weakness for chocolate.

Nutrition Analysis. The school lunch is certainly nutritious and worthy of a five-star rating. It contains all of the food groups, offers no items from the fats, oils, and sweets category, provides fresh fruit, and offers low-fat milk and lean meat in the spaghetti sauce. But even though her lunch was nutritionally balanced, it lost one star because Denise traded most of it and missed out on many important nutrients.

How to Raise Her Lunch Grade. If the school-lunch ordering policy in your school can't be changed, it's a good idea to pack nutritious extras on days when your child doesn't like what's served. Try going over the menu beforehand to see what your child won't eat, then send food-group-related items in their place. For example, if your child won't eat the fruit that's offered, send something she likes, such as an orange or some fresh strawberries. And if your child has a weakness for chocolate, as Denise does, pack a bite-size candy bar, or let her order chocolate milk to help her resist the temptation of trading her entire lunch for something chocolaty and sweet.

True or False? Chocolate Milk Is Loaded with Sugar and Caffeine.

False. Although this is a *loaded* question, chalk one up for chocolate milk. While chocolate milk does have some sugar and caffeine, it's only a small amount; and, like white milk, chocolate milk contains nine essential nutrients, including protein, calcium, and vitamin D. In comparison to other sweet drinks, chocolate milk has two fewer teaspoons of sugar per eight-ounce serving than a soft drink (which has no nutrients) and less sugar than a juice drink. Also, the amount of caffeine in a cup of chocolate milk (two to seven milligrams) is similar to the amount found in decaffeinated drinks (colas contain up to ten times more caffeine than chocolate milk.)

BANISHING BROWN-BAG BOREDOM

While it's important to send your child to school with a nutritious lunch, all of your good intentions and efforts will have been in vain if your child doesn't eat it. To ensure that your child's lunch makes it into her stomach (and not someone else's), check out the following strategies.

Top Ten Tips for Getting Kids to Eat Their Lunch

1. *Sit down once a week and plan lunches together.* Then encourage your child to pack his own lunch. If kids have a vested interest in their lunch, they're more likely to eat it.
2. *Let them play before they eat.* Studies have found that grade-schoolers will eat more and waste less if they have recess *before* lunch. Talk with your principal or school board to see if this is a possibility for your child's school.
3. *Celebrate special days.* Plan lunch menus around a special event. For example, pack an all-red lunch in honor of Valentine's Day, or include a fortune cookie to celebrate Chinese New Year. For a decorative touch toss a red-and-white-checked napkin into your child's lunch box to create a picnic-like atmosphere.
4. *Try new food products.* Send exotic fruits like kiwi or carambola (star fruit). Or go ahead and buy that new food your child saw advertised on television. Even if it's not a nutritional winner, remember that all foods have their place in a healthy diet, when eaten in moderation.
5. *Slip them a note.* A simple note saying "I think you're great!" written on a sheet of paper or a banana peel, or a special poem in your child's lunch box can help make his day.
6. *Make your own happy meals.* Include a sticker, joke, or small toy in your child's lunch. This is always a real hit with younger grade-schoolers.

7. *Invest in "cool" lunch equipment.* An insulated lunch bag and a thermos will enable your child to take a wider variety of foods for lunch, such as chilled pasta salad or hot soup.

8. *Send favorite foods.* If your child loves certain foods, such as apples, pretzels, or low-fat yogurt, go ahead and pack them. If she prefers leftover chicken legs, cold pizza, or single-serve boxes of cereal to a sandwich, send those to school, too.

9. *Give them a treat.* Occasionally include items like cookies, chips, and bite-size candy bars. But be sure to pack only a small amount, so that your child doesn't fill up on the treats and skip the rest of his lunch.

10. *Pack extras to share with friends.* If you're trying to get your child to eat something new, like celery stuffed with peanut butter, take advantage of the power of peer pressure and pack a few extra items for the other kids to taste.

The Four Hottest School Lunches

According to the American School Food Service the most popular selling lunches are:

1—Pizza (It's so popular, it's almost as if there is no second place.)

2—Chicken (typically nuggets)

3—Mexican foods (tacos)

4—Hamburgers

Although these school lunches may sound like high-fat fast foods, they're healthier than typical fast-food options. Because of the School Meals Initiative for Healthy Children, the pizza and tacos are made with reduced-fat cheese. The chicken nuggets and patties are baked rather than fried. And the hamburgers are made with lean beef.

WHAT'S FOR LUNCH?

One of the best ways to expedite the lunch-making process is to stock up on nutritious and delicious foods. Keep your refrigerator and pantry filled with items that either you or your child can easily assemble into a quick and healthy lunch. Here are some foods you'll want to keep on hand.

How to Stock a Lunch Bar

Put some of these foods in your refrigerator:

Grain Group: whole-grain tortillas

Vegetable Group: salsa; grated and baby carrots; bell peppers; cucumbers; prewashed spinach and salad bags; alfalfa sprouts; tomato juice

Fruit Group: fresh fruit such as mangos, oranges, pears, and apples; cranberry relish

Dairy Group: low-fat milk; low-fat yogurt; shredded, string, sliced, and cubed cheeses; grated Parmesan cheese; chocolate milk; pudding made with reduced-fat milk

Protein Group: lean luncheon meats such as turkey, ham, roast beef, and reduced-fat salami; hard-boiled eggs

Stock your freezer with these foods:

Grain Group: cinnamon-raisin bagels; whole-grain pita bread; whole-grain dinner rolls and buns

Vegetable Group: frozen mixed vegetables; chopped bell peppers; chopped onion

Fruit Group: melon balls; berries like blueberries and strawberries

Protein Group: lean luncheon meats such as turkey, ham, and roast beef

Make sure your pantry is filled with these foods:

Grain Group: whole-wheat bread; dry pasta; bread sticks; whole-grain crackers

Vegetable Group: single-serve cans of vegetable juice; tomatoes;
tomato juice

Fruit Group: bananas; canned fruit cups packed in natural juice;
100 percent fruit juice

Protein Group: cans of fat-free refried beans; reduced-fat peanut
butter and other nut butters; cans of soup like chicken noodle
and beef vegetable; tuna canned in water; garbanzo beans

Fats, Oils, and Sweets Category: reduced-fat and fat-free salad
dressings; fat-free mayonnaise; bite-size candy bars; jelly

Playing It Safe

To prevent your child's lunch—and appetite—from spoiling, here
are some lunch-packing food-safety guidelines you'll want to follow.

Purchase a good thermos. A stainless-steel thermos is the best
insulator, but it's heavier and more expensive than a plastic one. For
maximum chill, store the thermos overnight in the refrigerator. And
invest in a lunch box or insulated lunch bag designed to keep food
either hot or cold.

Use an ice pack in your child's lunch box. You can make your own
by simply freezing a 100 percent fruit juice box, then packing it in
your child's lunch. It will thaw gradually and keep food cool. You can
also keep your child's lunch cool by making a sandwich with frozen
bread; it too will thaw by lunchtime. But pack the lettuce and
tomato for the sandwich separately so the bread won't get soggy.

Keep it clean. Wash containers, lunch boxes, and reusable lunch
bags thoroughly with soap and warm water after each use, and
always throw away any leftover lunches.

LUNCH EXPRESS

One of the greatest challenges families face on school mornings is
deciding what to pack for lunch. But preparing brown bag lunches
doesn't have to be a chore. Here are some quick meal ideas that use

all of our "How to Stock a Lunch Bar" suggestions, *and* meet our Five-Star Lunch Criteria. Although kids of all ages will enjoy eating these lunches, any meal with a (★) may be more appealing to an older grade-schooler.

Big Easy Bean Burrito★ Spread fat-free refried beans on a whole-grain tortilla. Sprinkle with reduced-fat Monterey Jack cheese, and fold up ends together to make a burrito. Pack a small container of salsa to dip the burrito into, and add a sliced mango and a carton of low-fat milk.

Bagel Mania Top a cinnamon-raisin bagel with reduced-fat peanut butter and banana slices. Pack some baby carrots and let your child order a carton of low-fat chocolate milk from the school-lunch menu.

Wrap and Roll Place a thin layer of turkey, reduced-fat Swiss cheese, and several spinach leaves on a whole-grain tortilla. Top with cranberry relish, then wrap and roll. Serve with a small bottle of vegetable juice and a Granny Smith apple.

Some Like It Hot Fill a thermos with some minestrone soup. Add some whole-grain crackers, an orange, and a carton of low-fat milk.

Stuffed to the Tee Fill a whole-wheat pita pocket with tuna salad (made with fat-free mayonnaise), alfalfa sprouts, and grated carrots. Pack a pear and a carton of low-fat chocolate milk, and be sure to keep it cool.

It's a Toss-up★ Pick up a single-serve ready-to-eat salad bag with low-fat dressing from the grocery store. Pack some turkey luncheon meat and cheese cubes. Add a whole-grain dinner roll and a 100 percent fruit juice box.

Pastabilities★ Add some low-fat salad dressing to cooked pasta. Toss in some cherry tomatoes, chopped bell peppers, sliced olives, and grated Parmesan cheese. Serve with some breadsticks and a carton of low-fat milk.

Lunch Kebabs Skewer chunks of ham, turkey, cheese, melon balls, and cucumber slices on wooden skewers. Serve with whole-grain crackers and a carton of low-fat chocolate milk.

You're My Hero★ Create a super-tasting sub by filling a whole-grain bun with lean roast beef, reduced-fat salami, provolone cheese, tomato slices, and shredded lettuce. Add a canned fruit cup and carton of low-fat milk.

Planned-Over Pizza Save a few extra slices of veggie and cheese pizza from the previous night's supper. Pack a red delicious apple and carton of low-fat chocolate milk.

Lunch Box Specials

On weekend days when you have a few minutes to prepare a little extra something for your child's lunch, give one of these kid-friendly recipes a try. Better yet, double the recipes so you can send the leftovers to school with your child for her noontime meal.

◆　◆　◆

Algebra Soup

makes 8 servings

1　14-ounce can stewed tomatoes, undrained
3　10-ounce cans chicken or beef broth
1　10-ounce package frozen mixed vegetables
½ teaspoon basil
¼ teaspoon pepper
¼ cup number-shaped pasta, uncooked

Place tomatoes in a large saucepan, and mash with a potato masher. Add the broth, frozen vegetables, basil, and pepper, and stir well. Place over medium heat, and bring to a boil. Add the pasta, cover and reduce the heat. Simmer about 20 minutes.

◆ ◆ ◆

Nuts-and-Bolts Pasta Salad

makes 6 to 8 servings

8   ounces tricolor corkscrew pasta (fusilli)
8   ounces wheel-shaped pasta (rotelle or rotini)
½ cup black olives, halved
1   green bell pepper, chopped
1   red bell pepper, chopped
8   ounces of your child's favorite reduced-fat salad dressing
¼ cup grated Parmesan cheese

Cook the pasta according to package directions. Drain, and set aside to cool. Meanwhile, chop the olives and peppers. Once the pasta is cool, toss the pasta, olives, peppers, Parmesan cheese, and salad dressing together.

◆ ◆ ◆

EXTRA-CREDIT ASSIGNMENT

Beyond Peanut Butter and Jelly (PB&J)

If you and your child are in a PB&J lunch rut, then this assignment is a must. Together with your child, add variety to the sample menu by changing one food group each day. After you are all finished, you'll have a week's worth of five-star school lunches just waiting to be packed and eaten. If you need some help with food groups and recommended serving sizes, check out Chapter 2, Nutrition *Fun*damentals.

SAMPLE MENU

PB&J Sandwich:

   2 tablespoons of peanut butter (protein group) and
   1 teaspoon jelly (fats, oils, and sweets category) on
   2 slices of white bread (grain group) with
   1 small bag of baby carrots (vegetable group) and
   1 red apple (fruit group) and
   1 8-ounce carton of milk (dairy group)

Monday: Change the grain group serving to

_____

Tuesday: Change the vegetable group serving to

_____

Wednesday: Change the fruit group serving to

_____

Thursday: Change the dairy group serving to

_____

Friday: Add another protein group serving

_____

CHAPTER 5

Family Dinners in a Flash

◆ ◆ ◆

My mom makes the best macaroni and cheese—
it comes right out of a box!
—KAREN, SECOND GRADE

My parents both work late, so we eat lots of take-out foods,
like pizza and Chinese.
—ANGELA, THIRD GRADE

On the nights we have hockey practice we eat dinner
in our minivan.
—TREY, SIXTH GRADE

Top Three Dinner Mistakes Parents Make:

1. Don't sit down and eat together as a family.
2. Leave meal planning to the last minute.
3. Believe dinner takes too much time to prepare.

When it comes to eating dinner, everybody loves sitting down to a home-cooked meal. But let's face it, families today are so busy that there's little time to prepare dinner and even less time to sit down, relax, and enjoy a civilized meal. In this chapter you will:

- discover why grade-schoolers who regularly eat meals with their family tend to be happier, healthier, and smarter both in and out of the classroom;
- plan a meal that meets our Five-Star Dinner Criteria and uses several convenience and take-out foods;
- learn how to assemble a variety of nutritious dinners that can be on your table in 30 minutes or less.

WHATEVER HAPPENED TO THE FAMILY DINNER HOUR?

Contrary to popular opinion, the family meal is not extinct. (Although for some families it may be on the endangered species list!) In fact, the concept of family dining is alive and kicking: American families are eating dinner together on an average of four to five times a week, according to a recent national survey conducted for the National Pork Producers Council. However, another study conducted by researchers at Harvard Medical School, Massachusetts General Hospital, and the Harvard School of Public Health found that children tend to eat dinner far less frequently with their families as they get older.

So why, in our time-crunched society, should families make the effort to keep the family meal tradition alive? Several studies have shown that when families eat dinner together regularly, both the parents and kids benefit. Parents have the chance to spend more quality time with their family; the kids fare better physically, emotionally, and intellectually. So if your family dinner hour is constantly being bumped by other activities like soccer practice or volunteer meetings, here are ten good reasons why you may want to reconsider and make eating supper together a family affair.

If your family eats dinner together regularly you will . . .

1. *Keep the lines of communication open.* Eating dinner together provides a perfect opportunity for everyone to share information and ideas, such as what's going on at school, or where to go on the next family vacation. And it's a great way to help family members discuss disappointments and conflicts, such as not making the cheerleading squad or not being able to watch a PG 13 movie that all their friends have seen.

2. *Strengthen your family bond.* Eating dinner together is the glue that holds many families together. It's a ritual that gives everyone a chance to talk with and listen to each other and provide encouragement to one another.

3. *Bolster kids' self-confidence.* Studies have reported that children who eat dinner regularly with their family feel more secure and stable than those whose families have no established dinner routine.

4. *Offer some nutritional insurance.* Research shows that kids who eat dinner with their family tend to eat a wider variety of foods and are more likely to meet their daily nutritional requirements than those who eat without their parents present.

5. *Enhance vocabulary skills.* One study found that preschoolers who listened to and took part in extended conversations during dinner had higher vocabulary scores by age seven than children who didn't. And these same children turned out to be better readers and writers as well.

6. *Boost test scores.* Students who regularly share meals with their family score higher on academic tests than those who don't, according to a recent *Reader's Digest* survey.

7. *Broaden their eating horizons.* Researchers at the University of Illinois found that children are more likely to eat foods that they see their parents eating. But be patient: the researchers also learned that it takes at least ten tries before many youngsters will even taste a new or unfamiliar food.

8. *Practice table manners.* Children are socialized into adulthood at the family dinner table. They'll learn everything from using a napkin properly to clever ways to strike up a conversation—or get a word in—with others.

9. *Help kids just say no!* The teenagers least likely to use drugs are those who eat dinner with their family five or more nights a week, according to a survey from the National Center on Addiction and Substance Abuse.

10. *Let the good times roll.* Research aside, what could be better than sharing a meal at night with the people you love most?

ALL TOGETHER NOW—SECRETS OF SUCCESSFUL FAMILY MEALS

Now that you understand the importance of eating regularly scheduled meals with your family, your next mission, should you choose to accept it, is to get your spouse and kids to bite into the idea. But when all of you are pulled in so many directions at the same time with hectic work schedules, Little League games, school meetings, book reports, etc; how can you possibly squeeze dinner in every night? Here are some strategies that have helped put dinner on the table in our homes most nights of the week, and better yet, made it an experience worth repeating. No matter which strategy (or strategies) you choose, keep in mind that the key to successful family meals boils down to planning, simplicity, and convenience.

Communicate the date. Pull out the family calendar and, along with your family, pencil in what time dinner is going to be served each night. This will make eating together more of a priority. But remember: Dinner doesn't need to be served at the same time each night; the key is that *everyone is able to attend.* If eating together *every* night is too overwhelming, aim for two nights a week, and add more family meals over time.

Plan meals in advance. To avoid that last-minute "What's for dinner?" syndrome, once a week jot down some meals that your whole family would like to eat. Family input is key in helping to relieve the time-dependent chef of comments like, "I don't like that!" Also, use the Food Guide Pyramid to help you plan your menus, and try to offer at least one food from each of the food groups (see Chapters 2 and 8).

Put Their Manners to the Test!

You don't have to wait for a special occasion to teach your child table manners. Try to keep the atmosphere positive, and practice, practice, practice using these tips:

- *Where does the fork go?* Start with a simple table setting, with a fork on the left and a knife (sharp edge facing toward the plate) and spoon on the right; the glass goes on the right above the knife and spoon. On Sunday, add a salad fork (place it to the left of the entree fork) and a soup spoon (next to the regular spoon).
- *"Mabel, Mabel . . . get your elbows off the table."* Your kids may be familiar with this saying, but how about never reaching across the table, or leaving their silverware on their plate when they're done eating? Good table manners may take some time to establish, but they will last a lifetime.
- *It's a bird, it's a plane . . . it's a napkin!* Encourage your children to place their napkin on their lap. And for fun, let them try folding their napkins into a creative creature like a swan or a plane.
- *Light up their lives.* Create a soothing ambience by using candles and playing soft music. Soon everyone will feel relaxed after a long day and will partake in the conversation.
- *"Thank you, sir. May I have another?"* Remind your kids to say please, thank you, and may I be excused?

Keep it simple. Use prepackaged products like pasta sauces and ready-to-eat salads, or create a buffet of leftovers when you're in a hurry.

Be a "taskmaster." When preparing the evening meal, adults can be in charge of the entree, older kids can toss a salad, and little ones can set the table. With everyone pitching in, there's more time for catching up with one another.

Disconnect distractions. Make conversation part of the dining experience. Tune in to your family by turning off the television set and letting the answering machine pick up phone calls.

THE DINNER DILEMMA

Congratulations! Your family has agreed to give eating dinners together a try. But chances are, you're puzzling over the answer to the age-old question: What are we going to eat? To help you work through this dilemma, we've revised our Five-Star Dinner Criteria from Chapter 4: Lunch Lessons. In order for a dinner to be considered balanced, it still must earn a rating of five stars, but we've now added emphasis on reducing the time element involved with preparing dinner.

Five-Star Dinner Criteria

A dinner should receive one star for meeting each of the following five criteria.

- ★ The dinner provides at least one selection from each of the five food groups.
- ★ It contains no more than one item from the nutritionally lacking fat, oils, and sweets category.
- ★ It includes high-fiber foods like whole-grain breads and cereals, vegetables, fruits, dry beans, nuts, and seeds.
- ★ Its fat content has been reduced.

★ *New!* The meal can be prepared in thirty minutes or less, and your child actually ate and enjoyed the dinner.

Sample Five-Star Dinner

Here's an example of a balanced dinner that meets our criteria, and that has met with our kids' overwhelming approval.

Sample Dinner Menu. Mediterranean chicken breast (a boneless, skinless chicken breast baked for twenty minutes with lemon juice and a pinch of oregano and topped with feta cheese); steamed broccoli; toasted whole-grain pita; vanilla low-fat yogurt topped with fresh berries; a glass of low-fat milk.

Nutrition Analysis. Let's review why this dinner meets our criteria.

It contains all five food groups: whole-grain pita = grain group, broccoli = vegetable group, fresh berries = fruit group, feta cheese, vanilla low-fat yogurt, and low-fat milk = dairy group, and chicken breast = protein group.

There are no servings from the fats, oils, and sweets category.

The whole-grain pita, broccoli, and fresh berries all provide fiber.

Attempts were made to lower the fat content; for instance, the skin was removed from the baked chicken breast, and it was baked, and the yogurt and milk were both low in fat.

The meal takes only thirty minutes to prepare, and we'll assume that everything was devoured.

DINNER-MENU REVIEW

If you apply our criteria to your dinner-planning endeavors, you'll be on the way to serving quick and nutritious meals. But just for a reality check, let's apply our Five-Star Dinner Criteria to some of the most popular dinner options for families and see how these meals stack up. In addition, we'll show you how to maximize the nutritional value of each meal and minimize your cooking time.

The TV Diner

1 TV frozen dinner, which included:
8 fried fish sticks
½ cup mashed potatoes with butter
½ cup corn
1 12-ounce can of cola
Total meal preparation Time = 15 minutes
Rating ★★

The Collins family, from Chicago, Illinois, has two very active boys: Brian, who is in sixth grade, and Brett, who is in third grade. Because the family has so many things going on after school such as soccer practice, basketball games, art class, and homework, there's very little time to eat, let alone cook. And because their dad often arrives home from work before their stepmom, he usually pops a frozen dinner in the microwave, and the boys eat while watching one of their favorite televison shows.

Nutrition Analysis. The boys' dinner was missing three of the five food groups: grain, fruit, and milk. Because it included butter and a cola, it contained more than one serving from the fats, oils, and sweets category. And even though the main course was fish, it was breaded and fried and no other attempts were made to lower the fat content. So the Collins's meal earned only two stars, one because the corn was a good source of fiber and the other, because it took only minutes to make and both boys ate it.

How to Raise Their Dinner Grade. Many families share the Collins's time-crunch dilemma. But because you have such little control over the ingredients in premade frozen meals, you're better off making your own. On days when you have more time to cook, make an extra batch of food and freeze it for future use. If you opt to purchase frozen dinners, look for meals that are labeled "healthy" or "reduced-fat." Another option is to purchase a frozen entrée, then add all of the trimmings, like a whole-grain dinner roll, tossed salad, fresh fruit, and a glass of low-fat milk. As for eating while watching TV, turn off the tube, and ask everyone to sit down together and talk about their day (see Chapter 9 for more about children and television).

How to Get Your Child Hooked on Fish

Most adults regard seafood as grown-up food, but studies show that kids can benefit from eating fish, too. Not only is seafood an excellent source of protein but it's also naturally low in fat, saturated fat, cholesterol, and sodium. What's more, it's rich in omega-3 fatty acids, a type of polyunsaturated fatty acid that may help lower blood cholesterol and prevent the incidence of heart disease later in life. Health experts recommend that everyone, including kids, eat fish at least once or twice a week. Here are a few tips to get your child to "bite" into seafood and lure them toward a lifetime of heathy eating:

- *Start early, and keep on trying.* Most of us develop our life-long eating habits during childhood. If you offer fish to your child when she's young, she is likely to acquire a taste for it and continue to eat it as she grows.
- *Balance texture and flavor.* Younger children often prefer fish with a soft texture and mild flavor such as cod, catfish, scallops, or shrimp. Older kids may enjoy fish with more texture and flavor, like swordfish or tuna.
- *"Sneak" fish into tried-and-true dishes.* Adding seafood to recipes that your child already likes increases the odds that he'll enjoy eating it. For example, try adding fish (or shell-fish) to your child's favorite soup, salad, or pasta dish.

Meat and Potatoes Meal

1 fried pork chop
20 french fries (frozen, then baked)
1 slice white bread with butter
½ cup applesauce
1 cup chocolate milk
Total meal preparation time: 60 minutes
Rating ★★

The Boston family, from Little Rock, Arkansas, have one son, Justin, who's in first grade, and preschool-age twin daughters. Justin's dad is an electrician who works long hours, so Justin's mom likes to make hearty meals for her hungry husband and family. Justin loves meat and potatoes but doesn't care for fruit.

Nutrition Analysis. The Bostons' dinner earned two stars because it was nutritionally balanced and included servings from all of the food groups, and it contained only one serving from the fats, oils, and sweets category (butter). It was lacking in fiber, however, and loaded with fat, and even though Justin ate it all, it took more than thirty minutes to make.

How to Raise Their Dinner Grade. While it's great that the Bostons' supper is balanced, it would be beneficial to scrap some of the fat and trim meal preparation time. Mrs. Boston could marinate pork loin chops (which are a leaner cut of pork) in a sauce like teriyaki, and use a quick, low-fat cooking method, like grilling or broiling, which helps the fat drip away from the meat. Instead of a high-fat vegetable, like french fries, she could serve a "baked" potato cooked in the microwave to save time. She should also encourage Justin to drink low-fat chocolate milk. To help boost fiber, she could serve whole-wheat bread and fresh apple slices. But if Justin really wants applesauce, that's okay, too, just as long as his mother buys an unsweetened brand to keep added sugars to a minimum.

Italian "Chow"

1 cup spaghetti
½ cup bottled pasta sauce
4 frozen meatballs, baked
1 piece Italian bread
1 cup low-fat milk
1 100 percent fruit juice pop
Total meal preparation time: 25 minutes
Rating ★★★★

The Massis, from Brooklyn, New York, are a busy family with Anna, a sophomore in high school; Alisa, who's in fifth grade; and Andrea, who's in kindergarten. All of the girls enjoy dancing, singing, and sports. Their mom feels it's important to serve balanced meals but feels guilty because she takes shortcuts such as using pasta sauce from a jar, frozen meatballs, and store-bought bread, instead of preparing a traditional Italian meal.

Nutrition Analysis. The Massi dinner is truly balanced; it includes servings from all of the food groups and no servings from the fats, oils, and sweets category. In addition, Mrs. Massi has attempted to reduce the fat in the meal by serving low-fat milk. And one of the biggest pluses of all is that she took meal preparation short-cuts to save time and the girls enjoyed eating their dinner. The only thing that prevents it from earning all five stars is that it is rather low in fiber.

How to Raise Their Dinner Grade. There's no need for Mrs. Massi to feel guilty: very few of us have time to make anything from scratch. But to help boost the fiber in this traditional Italian dinner, she could serve whole-wheat pasta noodles instead of regular spaghetti. Another great way to add fiber and nutrients is to add some vegetables to the pasta sauce, like chopped bell peppers and onions or frozen peas and carrots. A tossed salad or even some sliced fresh fruit or seasonal berries will add extra crunch and fiber. If Mrs. Massi is really feeling adventurous, she may want to go meatless by skipping the meatballs and tossing some cannellini beans (white kidney beans) into the sauce.

SOMEONE'S IN THE KITCHEN . . . BUT NOT FOR LONG!

When it comes to preparing dinner, everybody loves a home-cooked meal, but busy parents want to spend less time in the kitchen and more time at the dinner table with their families. Here are some shortcuts you can take so you can enjoy time with your family and a healthy, tasty meal in minutes. But if you simply must resort to a fast-food meal, check out Chapter 7: Extracurricular Eating for some quick picks that meet our Five-Star Criteria.

- *Stock up on nutritious standbys.* Keeping all the right ingredients on hand will guarantee a nutritious meal even on short notice. Make a list of frequently used items, and attach it to your refrigerator door. When you are running low on particular ingredients, replace them the next time you shop.
- *Use quick and easy cooking methods.* Stir-frying, sauteing, steaming, and cooking foods in the microwave are a few methods that are fast, cut back on fat, and help retain nutrients. For instance, you could stir-fry chicken tenders or sea scallops with an assortment of fresh or frozen vegetables, or steam rice and vegetables and top them with low-fat, shredded cheddar cheese.
- *Invest in the right cookware.* Treat yourself to some of the new cookware that's available to help the hurried cook. Steamers, nonstick pans, and microwave-safe dishes can definitely help you out in the kitchen. Woks or large, nonstick skillets with a lid are great for stir-frying. You may also want to consider a slow cooker such as a Crock-Pot to let soups, stews, and chili cook all day while you're out.
- *Combine what you're cooking.* Save yourself time whenever you can. Make boiling water do double duty. First add pasta, then

throw in frozen veggies for the last few minutes. Or prepare pork strips and rice together in the same skillet. Another idea is to saute vegetables with precooked chicken.

- *Double up your recipes.* Make an extra batch of lasagna or chili, then stash it in the freezer for another night. Or when you're cleaning and cutting fresh vegetables, bag and freeze some for next week's meal. Another smart idea is to simmer enough pasta for two days. Serve it hot with meat sauce one night, then chilled with tuna in a salad the next.

- *Plan for leftovers.* That beef and leftover rice you had on Monday can be used later in the week to make beef fajitas and stir-fried rice. Or one night's leftover chicken can be used to make a great Caesar salad the next night.

- *Prepare some items the night before.* As you're waiting for your noodles to boil, start preparing the next night's supper by removing the skin from precut chicken pieces and placing them in Zip-loc resealable plastic bags. That way all you have to do the next day is add some premade, bottled marinade, fire up the grill, and your family will be enjoying a hot meal in a matter of minutes.

- *Collect fast and healthy recipes.* Look for cookbooks or magazines that provide recipes that can be prepared in thirty minutes or less. Some sources also offer shopping lists, complete menu ideas, and suggestions for leftovers. The Internet is also a great place to look for recipes. Challenge your kids to browse the Web to find some quick dinner ideas, recipes, and nutrition tips.

- *Make cooking a family affair.* Cooking a meal together not only gets everyone involved but it can also entice kids to try new foods and bolster their self-esteem. Children are proud of what they make and receive immediate gratification once they've tasted their own creations. Learning to cook can also help improve their language skills (reading recipes), enhance their math skills (working with fractions), and turn them on to science (cooking really is chemistry). In addition, it can promote their future health. If children learn about nutrition and how to prepare food in tasty ways, they may end up eating more healthfully throughout life (see Chapter 8).

HOME-COOKED CONVENIENCE

If you want to gather your clan around the table each night for dinner, stop trying to live up to old-fashioned standards. The Brady Bunch style of elaborate homemade feasts are long gone. (Actually, their housekeeper cooked all of the meals!) Parents today don't have time to cook pot roast and bake bread. Dual careers, lengthy commutes, and unpredictable work schedules leave little time for preparing dinner. Time-pressed cooks are using convenience foods, prepared pasta sauces, frozen dinners, and canned soups to help them get dinner on the table in minutes. But, because many convenience foods are high in sodium and fat, and low in fiber, they've unfortunately earned a "not so healthy" reputation. As we have said many times throughout this book, all foods can fit into a healthy diet. The key is to eat a variety of foods, watch portion sizes, and balance food choices over the course of the week. Here are a few suggestions on how you can turn convenience foods into nutritional superstars.

Scan the food labels and compare products. Use the nutrition information on food labels to help you build healthy meals around convenience foods. Check out the labels of similar foods, and choose ones with less fat and sodium. You can also use the information on labels to help balance your child's diet. For example, let's say you're planning to serve macaroni and cheese for dinner. One look at the package label tells you that macaroni and cheese is a good source of calcium but also high in fat and low in fiber. Check the labels of other foods and choose complementary items that are low in fat and high in fiber, like frozen broccoli and whole grain dinner rolls (for more on label reading see Chapter 8).

Buy prepared grocery items to get a jump start on dinner. The new "speed scratch" trend (ready-to-eat foods) in supermarkets has helped make cooking as simple as possible. Supermarkets now offer freshly prepared items like salads in a bag and shredded or chopped vegetables that can be used to make a super-fast stir-fry. Other great time-savers include precooked shrimp, grated cheese, bags of frozen fruit, quick-cooking pasta, and prepared pizza crusts. You can also look for precut poultry and meat for kebabs, soups and stews. Often times these meats come in their own marinade. Here are a few Five-Star Dinners you can try that are made entirely with these quick-cooking ingredients:

1. Salad in a bag (add your child's favorite fat-free dressing); pizza made with a precooked crust and topped with grated part-skim milk mozzarella cheese, ready-to-eat-pizza sauce, reduced-fat salami, and precut veggies; fresh fruit cup packed in natural juice; and a glass of low-fat chocolate milk.

2. Grilled honey mustard chicken breast (that comes already marinated); ready-to-eat hash browns prepared with a hint of olive oil; baby carrots and low-fat dip; frozen fruit salad; whole-grain, brown-and-serve dinner roll; and a glass of low-fat milk.

3. Precut pork loin cubes stir-fried with prepackaged Oriental vegetables, presliced pineapple chunks, and a cup of Hoisin sauce; instant brown rice; and a pudding cup.

Enhance meal kits and convenience products with your own fresh ingredients. Packaged dinner mixes such as Hamburger, Tuna, and Chicken Helper® are popular quick-dinner options too. These kits come with the basics and require the addition of only one or two ingredients, such as vegetables and meat, but are often high in sodium and/or fat. The beauty of these kits, however, is that you can always "personalize" the meal and give it a healthier twist by adding leaner cuts of meat, extra vegetables, reduced-fat cheeses, and by reducing the amount of high-sodium seasoning that you use. For example, when making a hamburger box-mix meal, add extra lean ground beef or ground turkey (with the fat drained after cooking), sliced onions and bell peppers to boost fiber, and use about half of the season mix to reduce sodium. Or prepared a tuna-boxed meal using tuna canned in water to trim fat, add frozen pea pods to enhance fiber, and again use only half of the seasoning packet to trim sodium. When purchasing a single item convenience food, such as a dessert or salad, you can also add your own healthy touch. For example, add fresh or canned fruit to Jell-O for a nutritionally enhanced salad or dessert. Or you could always add more beans to frozen or canned chili, extra vegetables to canned soups, and grated carrots and chopped green peppers to pasta sauces.

Pick up a precooked dinner at your supermarket deli. Supermarkets now offer fully cooked ready-to-eat entrees such as rotisserie chicken, steamed shrimp, and deli sandwiches. You can even select the side dishes you want to have with these items. For a quick family-pleasing meal, pick up some tasty precooked items such as a baked chicken (or turkey breast) or a roasted pork loin. Then add a whole-grain salad like quinoa or couscous salad, roasted vegetables, and a side dish like baked beans, and serve fresh fruit salad for dessert.

Shop the salad bar. Help yourself to a cornucopia of precut fresh veggies from the supermarket salad bar. Bring home and serve them as a salad, or toss them into stir-fry dishes, soups, or stews. Or you could try serving them as is with a fat-free yogurt dip, or steam them until they're light crispy and sprinkle with fresh herbs.

Chill out and grab a frozen dinner for a quick no-hassle dinner. Rather than pick up single-serve frozen dinners for each family member, try serving one of the frozen meal-in-a-bag dinners that are available such as chicken, pasta, and vegetables, or beef stew, potatoes, and vegetables. They contain an entire meal for everyone, and they take only minutes to make. But the processing adds sodium and many do contain a great deal of fat. Look for brands that carry a "healthy" or "reduced-fat" claim on their package. And to help round out your meal so that it meets our Five-Star Criteria make sure that you fill in any nutritional gaps such as adding a whole-grain dinner roll, tossed salad with fat-free dressing, or piece of fresh fruit.

Add extra flavor with prepared seasonings. Seasoning mixes and marinades can get you started when making chili, stews, and meat loaf. But because some of these mixes contain a lot of sodium, remember to check out the label or use only half the package or bottle.

WEEKNIGHT SURVIVAL MENUS

To help you survive those hectic weeknights, we've come up with five healthy beat-the-clock menus that can all be prepared in fifteen minutes or less from the time you walk in the door. The recipes for each of the entrees are included. Plus, we've given you a complete shopping list to save you time in the supermarket. Some of the recipes can be made ahead of time and frozen. Others use quick-cooking methods and time-saving prepackaged foods. There's no need to follow the recipes exactly. Use the vegetables, grains, meats, or seasonings your family enjoys—in other words, just wing it!

Monday's Menu

Shrimp and vegetable stir-fry rice (recipe follows)
Fresh pineapple spears (available in the produce section of your grocery store)
Fortune cookies

Time-saving tip: Cook the rice in the morning while you're getting ready, then store it in the refrigerator.

◆ ◆ ◆

Shrimp and Vegetable Stir-Fry Rice
makes 6 servings

2 cups instant white or brown rice
nonstick cooking spray
1 8-ounce carton egg substitute
1 tablespoon canola oil
3 green onions, chopped
1 cup frozen peas and carrots, thawed
1 6- to 8-ounce bag of frozen salad-size shrimp, thawed under
   cold water
4 tablespoons low-sodium soy sauce

For fast cooking, prepare rice in your microwave oven according
to package directions. Coat a wok or large skillet with the nonstick cooking spray, and heat until a drop of water sizzles. Scramble the egg substitute in the wok, and set aside. Add the canola oil,
green onions, peas, carrots, and shrimp to the wok, and stir-fry
for about five minutes. Add the cooked rice, eggs, and soy sauce,
and stir-fry for about three minutes.

Tuesday's Menu

Crock-Pot veggie chili (recipe follows)
cheese quesadillas (place ¼ cup reduced-fat shredded cheddar
   cheese between two flour tortillas and bake at 350 degrees F for
   ten minutes)
mango slices

Crock-Pot Veggie Chili

makes 6 servings

Time-saving tip: Assemble the chili in the morning. It will slow-cook while you're on the go and be ready to eat when you walk in the door.

1   small onion, chopped
1   green pepper, chopped
1   15-ounce can pinto beans, drained and rinsed
1   15-ounce can black beans, drained and rinsed
1   15-ounce can kidney beans, drained and rinsed
1   6-ounce can tomato paste
2   8-ounce cans Mexican-style diced tomatoes
2 to 3 cups tomato juice
1   teaspoon chili powder
½ teaspoon cumin

Add all of the ingredients in the order listed above to a one-quart-size Crock-Pot. Cook on a low setting for at least eight hours or on a high setting for four hours. Variation: Add ½ pound cooked lean ground beef or turkey to the chili.

Wednesday's Menu

coo-chi couscous chicken tenders (recipe follows)
pita crisps (brush pita bread with olive oil, and bake at 425 degrees F for ten minutes)
frozen low-fat yogurt cone

Time-saving tip: Buy packaged pita crisps, or substitute focaccia bread.

◆ ◆ ◆

Coo-Chi Couscous Chicken Tenders

makes 6 servings

1 pound chicken tenders
¾ teaspoon garlic powder
2 teaspoons curry powder, divided in half
1 tablespoon olive oil
1 14-ounce can chicken broth
1 16-ounce package of mixed fresh vegetables (available in the
   produce department of your grocery store)
1 cup uncooked couscous
½ cup raisins

Place the chicken tenders in a medium bowl. Sprinkle with the
garlic powder and one teaspoon curry powder; toss to coat. Heat
the olive oil in a large, deep skillet over medium-high heat until
hot. Add the chicken to the skillet, and stir-fry for about five minutes or until the chicken is no longer pink in the center.

Transfer the chicken to a plate, and set aside. Add the broth,
mixed vegetables, and remaining curry powder to the skillet, and
bring to a boil over high heat. Cover with the skillet lid, and boil
for about two minutes.

Stir in the couscous and raisins, and top with the chicken;
cover, and remove from heat. Let stand for five minutes or until
the liquid is absorbed. Variations: Reduce the curry powder to
one teaspoon for a milder dish.

◆ ◆ ◆

Thursday's Menu

last-minute lasagna (recipe follows)
garlic bread (made with whole-grain bread)
red seedless grapes

Time-saving tip: Prepare this dish on a day when you have time to cook. Freeze the lasagna in individual portions, then, on the evening you want to serve it for dinner, microwave on the defrost cycle for about two minutes and on full power for three or four minutes.

◆ ◆ ◆

Last-Minute Lasagna

makes 6 servings

nonstick cooking spray
1 pound Italian turkey sausage
16 ounces reduced-fat ricotta cheese
4 egg whites, beaten
¼ cup grated Parmesan cheese
8 lasagna noodles, dry (there's no need to precook them, as they'll absorb the liquid from the sauce as they bake)
2 cups fresh spinach (use ready-to-eat salad bags)
16 ounces part-skim mozzarella cheese, shredded
2 26-ounce jars of your favorite pasta sauce

Preheat oven to 350 degrees F. Coat an 8" × 12" pan with the nonstick cooking spray. Brown the turkey sausage in a large skillet and drain the fat. Meanwhile, mix the ricotta cheese, egg whites, and Parmesan cheese together until well blended.

Next, layer half the lasagna noodles, cheese mixture, spinach leaves, turkey sausage, shredded mozzarella, and pasta sauce atop one another in the pan. Repeat the layers (in the same order), using the rest of the ingredients. Cover with aluminum foil, and bake for 45 minutes.

After the lasagna has cooled, cut into individual servings, and freeze. Heat the portions in the microwave as needed. Variation: For a meatless lasagna, omit the turkey sausage.

◆　◆　◆

Friday's Menu

deli-licious barbecue pork sandwiches (recipe follows)
corn on the cob (substitute frozen or canned corn, if you want)
watermelon wedges
low-fat milk

Time-saving tip: Pick up a precooked pork loin roast from your supermarket deli counter.

◆　◆　◆

Deli-licious Barbecue Pork Sandwiches

makes 6 servings

1　pound precooked pork loin roast
1　cup of your favorite barbecue sauce
1　small onion, chopped
1　green pepper, chopped
1　teaspoon olive oil
6　whole-grain hamburger buns

Slice the pork roast into sandwich-size slices. Place the pork slices in a microwave-safe bowl, and pour the barbecue sauce over the pork. Cover with plastic wrap, and microwave on a high setting for three minutes.

Saute the onion and green pepper in the olive oil for two minutes or until tender. Place the vegetables and the pork slices on a bun, and serve. Variation: Substitute chicken or turkey breast for the pork.

◆   ◆   ◆

Shopping List

Here's a complete shopping list of what you'll need to prepare your weeknight survival meals. Purchase a large package of each of the following ingredients so you'll have them on hand for your next quick meal:

Grain Group
instant brown rice
fortune cookies
flour tortillas (keep in refrigerator)
couscous
whole-grain pita bread (keep in freezer)
lasagna noodles
whole-grain bread and hamburger buns (keep in freezer)
1 package ice cream cones

Vegetable Group
1 bunch green onions
1 16-ounce package of peas and carrots, frozen
2 small onions
2 green bell peppers
1 6-ounce can tomato paste
2 8-ounce cans Mexican-style diced tomatoes
1 quart tomato juice
1 16-ounce package mixed vegetables
1 bag prepackaged spinach

2 26-ounce jars pasta sauce
6 ears corn on the cob

Fruit Group
1 bag pineapple spears, precut
1 bunch seedless red grapes
3 mangos
½ watermelon, presliced

Dairy Group
1 pound cheddar cheese, shredded
1 pound reduced-fat, part-skim mozzarella cheese, shredded
1 pint frozen yogurt
1 16-ounce container reduced-fat ricotta cheese
1 8-ounce package Parmesan cheese, shredded

Protein Group
1 8-ounce container egg substitute
1 6- to 8-ounce bag frozen salad-size shrimp
1 15-ounce can pinto beans, black beans, and kidney beans
1 pound chicken tenders
1 pound Italian turkey sausage
1 pound precooked pork loin roast

Fat, Oils, and Sweets Category
1 can nonstick cooking spray
1 large bottle canola oil
1 large bottle olive oil
1 large bottle low-sodium soy sauce
1 14-ounce can chicken broth
1 large jar barbecue sauce
1 container of: chili powder, cumin, curry powder,
   and garlic powder

EXTRA-CREDIT ASSIGNMENT

Table Topics

If your family is having trouble striking up a conversation at the dinner table, here's an activity you'll want to try. Ask your kids to develop a list of topics they would like to talk about at dinner. Have them write each topic on a piece of paper and place it in a basket. At dinner, take turns pulling out topics, and let the conversation begin!

Here are some conversation starters for younger grade-schoolers:

The funniest thing that happened at school today

Games you played at recess

Favorite foods to eat

What you want to be when you grow up

Older grade-schoolers may want to discuss these topics:

What did you like best about your family vacation?

Why did you like your favorite movie so much?

What makes a good friend?

What would you take with you if you traveled into space?

CHAPTER 6

After-School Snack Attacks

◆ ◆ ◆

My favorite after-school snack is called ants-on-a-log.
You take a glob of peanut butter and spread it on a
piece of celery; then you stick raisins on top.

—ANNIE, KINDERGARTEN

I have soccer practice right after school so I either bring a snack
or buy a candy bar at the nearby food mart.

—BILL, FOURTH GRADE

Both of my parents work so I make my own snacks.
They're usually something frozen, like a pizza,
so that I can nuke it in the microwave.

—TIM, SIXTH GRADE

**Top Three Snack Mistakes
Parents Make:**

1. Think snacking is a bad habit.
2. Let kids eat whatever they want.
3. Don't plan for snacks.

W hen your child arrives home from school, chances are she's *starving!* But is your grade-schooler *really* reaping the nutritional benefits from her snacking? That depends on whether she's nibbling on a bowl of cereal with low-fat milk or munching on chips washed down with a soda. *What* and *how much* your child chooses to nosh on, as well as *when* and *where* she snacks, can either make or break her daily diet. In this chapter you will:

- discover the nutritional benefits smart snacking has to offer grade-schoolers;
- determine your child's snacking style and how to provide snacks that appeal to her particular preferences;
- learn how to create a tasty snack that meets our Five-Star Snack Criteria and that's easy enough for your child to make.

SNACKIN'—JUST DO IT!

Believe it or not, snacking is actually good for kids, and it's important for grade-schoolers to eat at least one healthy snack every day. Their growing bodies require lots of calories and nutrients, which they often don't get from their three main meals. In fact, a recent government study found that snacks can contribute about 20 to 25 percent of the daily calories and nutrients kids need. Here are a few other good reasons why you should encourage, rather than discourage, your child to snack:

- *Snacks can boost your child's mental and physical skills.* If your child has music lessons that require concentration, or an after-school sports practice that requires a great deal of physical activity, a nutritious snack is a must. Studies have found that a midafternoon snack can help keep kids alert or improve their memory. And snacks that are eaten about two hours before a sport or physical activity can increase endurance and athletic performance.

- *Healthy snacks help fill in nutritional gaps.* Younger grade-schoolers have a smaller stomach capacity and find it difficult to finish their meal; older grade-schoolers are notorious for skipping breakfast and skimping on lunch. In both cases, an after-school snack can help provide calories (energy) and nutrients from food groups they might be missing.
- *Smart snacking may curtail overeating.* When chosen wisely, an after-school snack can help prevent your child from overeating at his next meal, especially if there's a large time lapse between lunch and dinner.

CHEW ON THIS

When it comes to snacks, some contain so much sugar and fat that they're more like "treats," which may be one of the reasons why snacking has received such a bum rap. In fact, according to a recent study conducted by researchers at the University of North Carolina–Chapel Hill, children between the ages of two and eighteen are eating greater portions of high-fat, sugar-laden treats like french fries, chips, cookies, candy, and soda, than they did twenty years ago. As a result, kids today are consuming more calories than in years past, which might explain, in part, why one out of every five youngsters in this country is overweight.

When weighing the benefits of snacks, parents should also be aware of *when* and *where* kids do their after-school snacking. Your best bet is to offer snacks at regularly scheduled times of the day, but at least one to two hours before your child's next meal. This will help take the edge off of her hunger without spoiling her appetite. You'll also want to designate a special place where you want your child to snack, preferably somewhere in your kitchen that is free of electronic distractions such as the television, telephone, or computer. When she's distracted, she's not focused on eating and can continue mindlessly munching long after she's no longer hungry.

Soft Drinks *Are* Hard on Kids' Diets

According to the latest U.S. Department of Agriculture data on the food habits of nearly ten thousand children nationwide, kids today are drinking more soft drinks than ever before. In fact, soft-drink consumption has increased 21 percent among two- to five-year-olds and 37 percent among six- to nine-year-olds in the past twenty years. Milk consumption, by contrast, has dropped 4 percent among preschoolers and 10 percent among six-to-nine-year-olds. Unfortunately, soft drinks provide kids with lots of calories but no nutrients, while milk has nine essential vitamins and minerals.

SMART SNACKS FOR GRADE-SCHOOLERS

Now that you're more aware of *why* snacks are important, you're probably wondering which snacks you should feed your grade-schooler. To help answer this question, we've developed what we call our Five-Star Snack Criteria. In order for a snack to be considered nutritious or balanced, it must earn a rating of five stars. You and your child can use the criteria to plan after-school snacks that can be eaten at home or on the go.

Five-Star Snack Criteria

A snack should earn one star for meeting each of the following five criteria. (See Chapter 2 for more detailed information about each of them.)

★ The snack provides at least one selection from two or more different foods groups.
★ It contains no more than one item from the nutritionally lacking fats, oils, and sweets category.
★ It includes high-fiber foods, like whole-grain breads and cereals, fruits, vegetables, dry beans, nuts, and seeds.

★ Its fat content has been reduced.

★ Your child actually helped prepare the snack, and then ate and enjoyed it.

Sample Five-Star Snack

Here's an example of a balanced snack, called Hot Potato, that meets our Five-Star Snack Criteria.

◆ ◆ ◆

Hot Potato*

*Recommended for the All-You-Can-Eat Aficionado
(we'll discuss this later in the chapter)

makes 1 serving

1 medium-size baking potato, scrubbed
½ cup canned turkey chili with beans
2 tablespoons grated reduced-fat cheddar cheese

Pierce the potato with a knife; place it on a paper towel in the microwave. Microwave on high for five minutes. Turn the potato halfway, and cook about five minutes more. Let the cooked potato stand about three minutes. Split the potato in half, and fluff with a fork.

While the potato is cooling, place the chili in a medium-size microwave-safe bowl; cover loosely with plastic wrap. Microwave the chili on high for three to four minutes or until thoroughly heated. Spoon the chili over the potato. Sprinkle with the cheddar cheese.

◆ ◆ ◆

Sample Snack Menu. 1 baking potato; ½ cup canned turkey chili with beans; 2 tablespoons grated reduced-fat cheddar cheese

Nutrition Analysis. Let's review why this snack meets our criteria.

It contains at least two different foods groups: potato = vegetable group, turkey chili with beans = protein group; cheddar cheese = dairy group.

There's no servings from the fats, oils, and sweets category.

The skin on the baked potato and the beans in the chili contain fiber.

The fat content has been lowered by using turkey chili and reduced-fat cheddar cheese.

Let's assume your child prepared the snack and ate it.

Say Cheese and Smile!

Frequently consuming sugary or starchy foods or drinks between meals such as candy, cookies, snack chips, and soft drinks places your child at a greater risk of developing cavities (dental caries). But because snacks are nutritionally important for grade-schoolers, here are a few pointers on keeping your child's teeth healthy.

- Make sure that your child brushes her teeth after eating snacks, or at least rinses her mouth out with water to help prevent food from sticking to the teeth.
- Offer snacks that are less likely to stick to the teeth, like yogurt or grapes.
- Encourage your child to snack on cheese; studies have found that it can help decrease the plaque build-up in your child's mouth and reduce her risk of developing cavities.

WHAT'S YOUR CHILD'S SNACKING STYLE?

How do actual kids' snacks compare to our Five-Star Snack Criteria? Curious to find out, we spent the day with Jodie's son, J.J., and his fifth-grade class. Not only did we learn which snacks kids eat, we were also brought up-to-date on when and where they like to eat them. Much to our surprise, we discovered that there are basically four snacking styles that seem to be the rage with today's grade-schoolers. To find out if your child's snacking habits fit one of the snacking profiles, answer the following questions. Then proceed directly to his particular style of snacking, and read how you can improve your child's snack choices so that they meet our criteria.

Questions. Circle all that apply to your child.

1. Fruit punch and french fries are your child's idea of snacking on fruits and veggies.
2. "Why can't I just eat a candy bar for a snack?" is a daily after-school mantra.
3. Most of your child's snacking takes place either in front of the TV or computer screen.
4. Snacking is more or less mindless munching because your child is typically doing something else such as chatting on the phone or cranking out homework while she's eating.
5. Your child is so busy after school that he barely has time for a snack.
6. Grab-and-go snacks work best for your child because they're easy to stash in a backpack or eat while dashing out the door.
7. When it comes to selecting snacks, your child prefers *quantity* over *quality*.
8. It's not uncommon for your child to raid the refrigerator when having an after-school snack attack.

How to Score. If you circled 1 and 2 . . . read the Junk-Food Craver.
    If you circled 3 and 4 . . . read the Mindless Muncher.

If you circled 5 and 6 . . . read the On-the-Go Snacker.

If you circled 7 and 8 . . . read the All-You-Can-Eat Aficionado.

If you didn't circle anything . . . congratulations! Your child snacks perfectly, so skip right to the recipes for great snack ideas.

If you circled several different responses . . . your child has a variety of snacking styles, so go ahead and read them all!

SNACKING STYLES

The Junk-Food Craver

1 giant-size chocolate bar

1 12-ounce can of cola

Rating: ★

Fifth-grader Mary Anne is a classic junk-food craver. This happens to be her favorite after-school snack, which she eats before heading off to gymnastics. She confesses that while her snack tastes great, she usually feels tired at the end of practice and can't wait until dinner.

Nutrition Analysis: Mary Anne's snack earned one star only because she did, in fact, make it herself and eat it. Technically, there is no such thing as "junk food"—even candy and soda can be part of a healthy diet when eaten in *small* amounts on *occasion*. Junk-food cravers have a tendency to snack on *large* amounts of these foods *on a frequent basis*. In fact, junk-food cravers often forgo the five food groups (grain, vegetable, fruit, dairy, and protein) and head straight to the top of the Food Guide Pyramid, to the fats, oils and sweets category, where they'll find foods with lots of calories and very few nutrients, like the ones Mary Anne enjoys. And even when kids with this snacking style select foods from the food groups, such as French fries or cookies, their choices tend to be loaded with fat or sugar. A common complaint from junk-food cravers is that their snack fills them up for only a short while.

How to Raise Her Snack Grade. If your child fits the junk-food craver profile, here's what you can do:

- *Keep junk foods out of sight.* Hungry kids will eat the snacks that are most readily available to them. Because kids get plenty of treats like candy and soda elsewhere (i.e., at parties and friends' houses) make it a policy to keep these foods our of your home.
- *Pay attention to protein.* Make sure that your child's snack contains at least two different food groups, with at least one food-group choice coming from the dairy or protein groups. Both of these groups offer excellent sources of protein, which takes longer to digest, and provides your child with the long-term energy she'll need to make it until dinner.
- *Have your child savor the sweet low-fat flavor.* To help satisfy your child's craving for sweets, offer low-fat snacks that are naturally sweet, like fresh seasonal berries and dried fruit. Or serve low-fat snacks that have only a small amount of added sugar, like chocolate milk, pudding, or vanilla yogurt.

Snack Suggestions for Junk-Food Cravers. Because the following foods contain protein and are naturally sweet, they would appeal to most junk-food cravers: low-fat yogurt with sliced strawberries, topped with low-fat granola; whole-grain toast with peanut butter and slices of banana; pasta salad with chopped vegetables and a glass of 100 percent fruit juice.

The Mindless Muncher

1 giant-size bag of buttered microwave popcorn
1 12-ounce squeeze bottle of fruit punch
Rating: ★★

Charlie, a bright techno-savvy fifth-grader, spends hours on the computer after school doing research and e-mailing his friends. Both of his parents work, so Charlie makes his own snack, which is typically something that's easy to eat while typing, like microwave popcorn. He also watches a lot of TV and often snacks while viewing his favorite programs. In fact, Charlie says he eats a lot of snacks because he always feels hungry.

Nutrition Analysis. Charlie's snack earned two stars: one because popcorn is a good source of fiber, and the other because he prepared and ate the entire snack. Unfortunately though, Charlie's snack contained only one food group (popcorn = grain) and all of the butter made it high in fat, which counts as a serving from the fats, oils, and sweets category. The fruit punch, which contains mostly sugar, falls into the same category as well. Mindless munchers are different from other snackers not necessarily because of *what* they eat but *where* they eat their snacks: in front of the TV, while playing video games, or while chatting on the phone. The bottom line is that mindless munchers do not pay attention to what, or how much, they're eating, and often overeat without ever feeling satisfied.

How to Raise His Snack Grade. If your child fits the mindless muncher profile, here's what you can do:

- *Tune out distractions.* Whether you're home or not, make it a rule that all snacks be eaten in a designated area like the kitchen table, and that the TV must be turned off and the answering machine turned on. Research has shown that it takes about twenty minutes for the brain to signal to the stomach that it's full and to stop eating.
- *Set electronic limits.* Kids who spend the greatest amount of time plugged into a television or computer tend to have a higher percentage of body fat than kids who spend time in more physical activities. The American Academy of Pediatrics encourages parents to limit their child's total "screen" time to no more than two hours a day. Encourage kids to go outside and play, or better yet, set an example and go out and play, too.
- *Keep snacks simple.* Remember the two-food-group-rule, and offer snacks that contain foods from a variety of groups. Keep plenty of nutritious ingredients on hand like whole-grain

crackers, baby carrots, fresh fruit, shredded low-fat cheese, and reduced-fat peanut butter, so that your child can quickly whip up a tasty, nutritious snack.

Snack Suggestions for the Mindless Muncher. The following snacks are particularly good for mindless munchers because they're quick to pull together and satisfying: baby carrots with yogurt dip and 100 percent fruit juice; scrambled eggs topped with salsa and low-fat cheese; mini bagels topped with fat-free cream cheese and a cherry tomato, and a glass of low-fat milk.

The On-the-Go Snacker

1 12-ounce bottle of water (only a few sips were swallowed)
1 package of chocolate cup cakes from the vending machine (but he didn't have time to eat them)
Rating: no stars

Kent, one of my son's best friends, always seems to be snacking on the run. After school he barely has time to finish his homework, let alone eat a snack, before he rushes off to hockey practice. In fact, many times he eats his snack in the car or buys something from the vending machine at the rink.

Nutrition Analysis. Kent's snack did not earn any stars because it met none of the Five-Star Snack Criteria. Busy family lifestyles coupled with kids' jam-packed activity calendars have made on-the-go snacking more common than ever. On-the-go snackers have difficulty with the *what, when,* and *where* of snacking because there never seems to be enough time to eat; they're always going somewhere like piano lessons, Little League practice, or dance class. And when they do eat a snack, it's typically something they can carry with them, or else they pick up whatever they can find on the way to their activity.

How to Raise His Snack Grade. If your child fits the on-the-go snacker profile, here's what you can do:

- *Make convenience key.* For a quick snack, always keep a stash of ready-to-eat foods available from each of the five food groups, such as whole-grain toaster waffles, prewashed baby carrots, fresh fruit, cartons of low-fat yogurt, string cheese, and reduced-fat peanut butter. You may also want to invest in prepackaged snacks like small bags of pretzels and granola bars, so your child can take them along with him.
- *Do some advance planning.* Prevent that last-minute after-school snack panic by spending a few minutes each week to plan your child's snacks in advance. Make sure the snack contains at least three food groups. Then write the snack on your family calendar as you're scheduling activities.
- *Know your options.* When forced to buy a snack on the run, opt for your lowest-fat choices. Many convenience stores offer deli sandwiches, pretzels, 100 percent fruit juice, and low-fat milk. Or swing by a coffee shop and pick up a bagel and cup of hot chocolate. Also, check out the chart for healthy picks from vending machines on page 123.

Snack Suggestions for On-the-Go Snackers: These nutrient-rich convenient snacks are a must for on-the-go snackers: Peanut butter and jelly on celery sticks and a thermos of low-fat milk; single-serve cans of tuna with whole-grain crackers and a drinkable yogurt; hard-boiled eggs, bread sticks, and a 100 percent fruit juice box.

Lean Vending Machine Cuisine

When you're trying to be a smart snacker nothing is more frustrating then being trapped by vending-machine selections. Here are some quick picks that will help fuel your child. Some may be a little higher in fat than others, but when your options are limited, they are often your best bet.

Grain Group: whole-wheat crackers, pretzels, popcorn, bagels, reduced-fat or baked tortilla chips, fig bars, oatmeal or peanut butter cookies

Vegetable Group: tomato or vegetable juice, vegetable soup, tossed salad, carrot sticks

Fruit Group: any fresh fruit, 100 percent fruit juice

Dairy Group: reduced-fat milk, yogurt, string cheese, pudding, ice cream or frozen yogurt

Protein Group: nuts or seeds, hard-boiled egg, bean dip, beef jerky

---

All-You-Can-Eat Aficionado

2 glasses of orange juice
1 pint chocolate-swirl ice cream topped with chocolate sauce
2 granola bars
Rating: ★★★★

Caitlin is an easygoing fifth-grader who skimps on breakfast because she's not very hungry in the morning. She also trades away most of her lunch since she often doesn't like what her parents pack. Consequently, she's ravenously hungry when she gets home from school. In fact, she's so hungry that she eats just about anything she can get her hands, and her mouth, on.

Nutrition Analysis. Caitlin's snack earned four stars because it consisted of at least two food groups: orange juice = fruit group, ice cream = dairy group, granola bars = grain group; her snack contained only one serving from the fats, oils, and sweets category (the chocolate sauce); the granola bars provided fiber; and she definitely made and ate it all. However, she made no attempt to reduce the fat content of the snack, and the portions were way too hefty. All-you-can-eat aficionados have fewer problems with *what* they eat and *where* they eat snacks; their biggest problem is with "portion distortion" or *how much* they eat. It's not unusual for kids with this snacking style to wolf down a dozen cookies or a pint of ice cream. Skipping meals is often the main culprit behind their after-school snack attacks. But some kids, especially during growth spurts, may eat all of their meals and still declare they're starving.

How to Raise Her Snack Grade. If your child fits the all-you-can-eat aficionado profile, here's what you can do:

- *Practice portion control.* Teach your child how to read food labels, and be sure to point out the serving size listed on the package. Or help your child visualize a portion size; for example, two tablespoons of peanut butter = the size of a golf ball; four small cookies = four casino chips; one medium orange or apple = the size of a baseball; one pancake or waffle = a four-inch CD.
- *Get kids involved.* Children are more likely to eat foods that they've helped prepare. Let your child make her own breakfast or pack her own lunch. Or go over the school menu in advance, and if there are foods she refuses to eat, send along a nutritious substitute that day.
- *Offer a variety.* To prevent your child from "pigging out" on a single food and missing out on a variety of nutrients, remind her to follow the two-food-group rule, which means that her snack must consist of at least two different food groups.

Snack Suggestions for All-You-Can Eat Aficionados: Any of these snacks would satisfy the hunger of the all-you-can-eat aficionados: toasted English muffin with pizza sauce and low-fat mozzarella cheese; scoop of frozen yogurt and a sliced banana between two graham crackers; a toasted whole-grain waffle capped with lemon yogurt and blueberries.

SAVVY SNACKS FOR HUNGRY KIDS

Help satisfy your child's after-school urge to splurge with these tempting treats. Each snack combo contains at least two food groups. Your snacker will not only enjoy eating them but because they're so quick and easy to prepare she'll be able to make them, too.

◆　◆　◆

"Cool" Veggie Pizza and Frosty Fruit Soda*

*Recommended for the junk-food craver

makes 1 serving

Pizza Ingredients
1 8-inch prebaked pizza crust
4 tablespoons fat-free cream cheese (tub style so it's easier to spread)
1 tablespoon dill-flavored spice blend
a variety of chopped veggies such as grated carrots, bell peppers, broccoli florets, and green onions

Spread the cream cheese evenly over the pizza crust and top with dill flavored spice blend and the chopped vegetables. Cut into pizza wedges and enjoy!

Frosty Fruit Soda Ingredients
1 cup vanilla- or fruit-flavored frozen yogurt
2 tablespoons frozen white grape juice concentrate
¾ cup sugar-free carbonated beverage like ginger ale or lemon-lime soda

Place the frozen yogurt at the bottom of a tall glass. Mix the frozen grape juice concentrate with the carbonated beverage, and pour into the glass over the frozen yogurt. Serve with a straw and spoon.

◆   ◆   ◆

Super-Easy Nacho Bites*

*Recommended for the mindless muncher

makes 1 serving

6   large baked low-fat tortilla chips
¼ cup shredded reduced-fat cheddar cheese
2   tablespoons fat-free refried beans
2   tablespoons chunky salsa

Arrange the chips in a single layer on a large microwave-safe plate. Sprinkle each chip with cheese. Spoon the beans over the chips, and top with the salsa. Microwave at medium power for one minute. Rotate the dish, and continue to microwave for another thirty to sixty seconds, or until the cheese is melted.

◆   ◆   ◆

High-Energy Smoothie with Banana Muffin*

*Recommended for the on-the-go eater

makes 2 6-ounce smoothies and 12 muffins

Smoothie Ingredients
½ medium banana, peeled
½ 8-ounce can crushed pineapple, packed in natural juice
½ 8-ounce carton low-fat vanilla yogurt
½ cup orange juice
6 to 8 ice cubes

Place all of the ingredients into a blender, and whir until well mixed. Pour into two cups, and start sippin'!

Muffin Ingredients
12   muffin cup liners
1½ cups all-purpose flour
½   cup quick-cooking rolled oats
⅓   cup brown sugar
1½ teaspoons baking powder
½   teaspoon baking soda
½   teaspoon ground cinnamon
4   egg whites
3   ripe bananas, mashed
½   cup canola oil

Place the muffin cup liners in the muffin tin compartments. Preheat the oven to 400 degrees F. Put the flour, rolled oats, brown sugar, baking powder, baking soda, and cinnamon in a large mixing bowl; stir with a wooden spoon until well combined. Place the egg whites into a medium-size bowl, and beat lightly. Add the oil and mashed bananas to the eggs, and beat with a fork until the wet ingredients are well mixed.

Add the egg mixture to the flour mixture. Stir with the wooden spoon until the dry ingredients are wet. Be careful not to overmix; the batter should be somewhat lumpy, not smooth. Spoon an equal amount of batter into each of the muffin cup liners. Bake about 20 minutes or until golden brown. Remove from the oven, and cool on a wire rack. Note: You can freeze the muffins for future use.

EXTRA-CREDIT ASSIGNMENT

Hey, Kids!
What's Your Snacking Style?

Go ahead. Ask your grade-schooler to take the Snacking Style quiz on page 117 and determine which profile fits him best. Then together come up with a list of after-school snack ideas. Have your child pick his top five favorites and write them in the spaces below.

1. _____

2. _____

3. _____

4. _____

5. _____

CHAPTER 7

Extracurricular Eating

◆ ◆ ◆

When I go to the movie theater, I always order
popcorn with lots of butter.
—JASON, SECOND GRADE

My friends and I think fast food rocks!
—JOHNNY, FIFTH GRADE

I love it when kids bring birthday treats to school,
especially cupcakes with gooey frosting.
—STACY, KINDERGARTEN

Top Three Mistakes Parents Make
When Their Kids Eat Out:

1. Order super-sized meals and snacks.
2. Don't teach them how to *balance* their
   food choices throughout the day.
3. Forget about healthy eating over the
   holidays.

T hroughout the grade school years, your child will have many opportunities to eat outside of your home, often without you around to supervise his choices. Will he eat smart? That all depends on you and how well you've prepared him for these "extracurricular" eating activities, and more important, the example you set for your child in similar eating situations. In this chapter you will:

- learn how to help your child pick the healthiest options available at fast-food restaurants and concession stands;
- find out how your child can have her birthday cake and enjoy eating it, too;
- discover how you can make your child's holiday spirits bright and eat light.

LIFE IN THE FAST-FOOD LANE

Everyone finds themselves in a time crunch once in a while, and fast food is a logical solution. On top of that, the moderate price of a fast-food meal fits the budget of many grade-schoolers eager to spend their allowance. So no wonder that a recent Gallup survey found that most Americans eat at fast-food restaurants eight or more times a month. While there is no set limit as to how often a child should eat fast food, moderation is key when it comes to healthful eating. As we've stressed throughout this book, all foods can fit in to a healthy diet. And with a little creativity even hamburgers and french fries can be included. But remember, fast foods do tend to be lower in the nutrients that are particularly important for growing children. Nutrients typically lacking in fast foods are:

- vitamins A and C, which help keep the skin soft and healthy, fight off infections, and heal cuts and broken bones;
- calcium, which is necessary to build strong bones and teeth;
- fiber, needed to help keep bowel movements regular (see Appendix A for more about specific nutrient functions).

By balancing how often your child eats fast food (and how much of it he eats), you'll be more likely to make fast eating healthy eating. Here are a few strategies for making fast food a healthy part of your child's diet:

Pace yourself. If you feel your family is eating at fast-food restaurants too often, try to pinpoint why. If you're short on cooking time, try keeping ingredients like spaghetti, pasta sauce, and Parmesan cheese on hand for quick and easy dinners. If there's absolutely no time to cook, plan ahead and pack a cooler with sandwiches, yogurt, and baby carrots for a meal on wheels in your car (see Chapter 5 for more fast dinner suggestions).

Keep things in perspective. Remember that a nutritious diet can't be created or destroyed by one meal. It's the *overall* pattern of food choices *over time* that counts. If your child is planning to have chicken nuggets, French fries, and a soft drink for dinner, make sure that the day's breakfast and lunch are significantly lower in calories, fat, and sodium.

Remember variety. Your child can get the forty-plus nutrients her body needs if she eats a variety of foods. One way to do this with fast food is to eat at different restaurants that offer different types of foods. For instance, go to a pizza place one time and go to a place that serves tacos the next. Or if your child insists on going to the same restaurant, encourage her to order different items each time.

Maximize food groups. A heathy diet requires making choices from each of the food groups. When ordering fast food, make sure your child selects items from each of the five main food groups, especially the vegetable, fruit, and dairy groups, which are more challenging to locate in fast-food restaurants. Here are a few regulars you'll find on most fast-food menus:

Grain Group: buns, tortillas, pizza crust, and crackers
Vegetable Group: tomato sauce, lettuce, potatoes, and grated carrots

Fruit Group: apple and orange juice, pineapple, and applesauce
Dairy Group: chocolate milk, frozen yogurt, and cheese
Protein Group: hamburger, pepperoni, ham, sausage, chicken, and
    refried beans
Fats, Oils, and Sweets (use sparingly): salad dressings, mayonnaise,
    butter, and soft drinks.

NUTRITION TIPS TO GO

Even though your family may be in a hurry to eat, don't overlook
nutrition. Teach your child the following tips so that he can order a
healthier, tastier fast-food meal.

Trim the fat (and calories)
    Think small, and order the regular-size hamburger and small
        french fries, rather than the super-deluxe size.
    Try broiled or grilled meat instead of fried.

Watch the toppings
    Add a dollop of mustard or a splash of low-fat salad dressing, and
        hold the mayonnaise and special sauces.
    Peel the skin off chicken.

Boost calcium
    Order a carton of low-fat milk.
    Request low-fat mozzarella cheese on your pizza, if it's available.
    Try a frozen yogurt shake or cone for dessert.

Pump up vitamins A and C and fiber
    Pile veggies like green pepper, mushrooms, and onions on your
        pizza.
    Ask for lettuce, tomato, and onion on your burger.
    Order a salad or baked potato instead of French fries.
    Add salad toppings such as pineapple, carrots, tomatoes, and
        broccoli.
    Try whole-grain buns or pizza crust.

Shake the sodium
 Request unsalted french fries.
 Balance your sodium intake for the day by eating less sodium at
  breakfast and lunch.

Burn it off
 Eat at restaurants that have playgrounds.
 Keep active by turning off the TV, then go out and shoot hoops,
  jump rope, or just move!

Quick Picks

When you're in a pinch, these are some fast-food meals you can
count on for a balanced meal. Sodium is difficult to limit at fast-
food restaurants, so on days when your child eats fast food, make
sure her other meals are lower in sodium. Each menu meets our
Five-Star Criteria for lunch and dinner (see Chapters 4 and 5).

Breakaway Burger
 Cheeseburger with bun (regular-size) topped with ketchup, mustard, pickle, and lettuce; french fries (small); and a small carton
  of orange juice

Fleeting Fowl
 Chicken nuggets (small serving), salad with low-fat dressing,
  frozen-yogurt cone, and a small carton of apple juice

Pronto Pizza
 Pizza (two slices) topped with ham and pineapple, and a carton
  of low-fat milk

The Speedy Gonzalez
 Bean burrito with salsa and cheese, cinnamon twists, apple
  (from home), and small diet soft drink

Fast-Food Facts

Have you ever wondered how much fat is in a serving of McDonald's Chicken McNuggets? Check out the following Web site at www.olen.com/food/ and you'll be able to determine the calorie, fat, and sodium content of some of your child's favorite fast foods. Also, all fast-food restaurants have nutrition information available where you order your food. If you don't see any, just ask for it.

CLOSE ENCOUNTERS AT THE CONCESSION STAND

Grade-schoolers love to visit fun places like museums, zoos, amusement parks, sporting events, and movie theaters to name just a few. But no matter where your child goes, there are sure to be the usual dietary temptations: hot dogs, french fries, potato chips, candy, and soft drinks. Not only are these concession-stand choices expensive but they're also loaded with fat and calories, and they're devoid of nutrients that kids need such as calcium and iron. While these foods are okay in moderation, it's better to reserve these treats for activities your family participates in every once in a while, like your annual trek to the state fair.

But rather than ban concession-stand foods altogether, help your child learn which ones are healthier options. Teach her to be a concession-stand connoisseur and to look for foods that fit into one of the food groups so that they pack a large nutritional punch. And encourage her to go easy on the fats and sugars. Some healthier concession-stand options include:

Grain Group: soft pretzels, popcorn (hold the butter), and whole-grain buns
Vegetable Group: chef's salad, corn on the cob, baked potato, salsa, and baked potato chips
Fruit Group: 100 percent fruit juice, raisins, and fresh fruit

Dairy Group: low-fat milk, frozen yogurt, and soft-serve ice cream

Protein Group: grilled chicken, turkey, or ham sandwiches without the mayonnaise, chili, peanuts, and sunflower seeds.

Take-Along Meals

One way to ensure that your child eats a nutritious snack or meal when she's out on the town is to plan ahead and have her take it along. That way she can bypass the concession-stand cuisine and she'll be in great shape for any on-the-go eating events. When you opt to bring your own, follow some of these guidelines for safe and pleasurable eating:

- Bring a cooler or insulated lunch bag to keep foods cold and to prevent them from spoiling.
- Take along prepackaged foods and drinks such as single-serve cereal, string cheese, individual bags of pretzels, or 100 percent fruit juice boxes. They're easy to serve and are more convenient to carry, and can even be tucked into a backpack or fanny pack.
- Offer your child plenty of water to keep her hydrated. You may want to take a water bottle with you. If treating your child to a soft drink, opt for a decaffeinated one.
- Caffeine has a diuretic effect and may dehydrate your child rather than quench her thirst.
- Pack beverages in plastic containers. These items are safer than glass and are acceptable at many places such as public pools, where glass containers are usually banned.

BIRTHDAY PARTIES THAT TAKE THE CAKE!

What makes kids happy at birthday parties? For some, it's the chocolate cake smothered in vanilla ice cream. For others, it's the goody bags bulging with candy. While these tasty treats are fine to eat every once in a while, kids can get overloaded with sweets if they go to a birthday bash almost every week (as our kids seem to do!). Before planning your child's next celebration, consider these pointers. They'll help you make your festivities a little less sugary, a tad healthier, and still a whole lot of fun.

Should You Let Them Eat Cake?

All foods, even cake, ice cream, and candy, have their place in a healthy diet. Remember that kids can eat anything they want in moderation, but they need to compensate for the extra calories elsewhere in their day. For instance, if you know your child will be eating cake and drinking soda at a party, plan to serve a light dinner afterward and hold off on dessert. You'll also want to strike a balance between what (and how much) your child eats and the amount of physical activity he gets (see Chapter 9 for more information on kids and physical activity). One way you can do this when hosting a birthday party is to focus on the fun rather than on the food. Here are a few tips that can help you get your guests rocking and rolling.

Pick an action-packed party theme. Have a pool party, take kids roller-skating, or host a mini-Olympics in your backyard or at a park.

Stage activities that keep your guests moving. Some all-time favorites include a game of duck, duck, goose; musical chairs; dance contests; and scavenger or treasure hunts.

Provide less-sweet and lower-fat munchies. Most kids love treats like popcorn, pretzels, apple slices with low-fat yogurt dip, taco chips and salsa, and 100 percent fruit juice punch. Set the treats out in small bowls or on trays for guests to nibble on or sip during the party.

Prepare quick and easy kid-favorite meals in more healthful ways. When making hamburgers or sloppy joes, use extra-lean ground beef and drain any excess fat. Or have kids make their own individual pizzas using English muffins or mini preprepared pizza crusts, shredded part-skim mozzarella cheese, and a dab of pizza sauce. Bake the pizzas for ten minutes, or until the cheese melts.

HEALTHY CAKES

A birthday party just wouldn't be the same without a cake. A cake signals that it's time to sing "Happy Birthday," make a wish, blow out the candles, and open the presents. But while most birthday cakes are laden with sugar and fat, they don't have to be. Try some of the following strategies for making your child's birthday cake both delicious and nutritious.

Find a tasty recipe, and try baking the cake from scratch. That way you can control the types of ingredients that go into your child's cake (see Chapter 8 for ingredient substitution ideas). Baking a homemade cake may take a little extra time, but the end result (taste and your child's health) are worth it.

Use reduced-fat cake mixes, or bake an angel food cake. Many of the reduced-fat mixes taste so good, none of your guests will know the difference. Angel food cakes are also a great choice because they contain less fat (they're made with egg whites) and lower amounts of sugar than other cakes.

Make tasty substitutions. Whether you bake from scratch or use a mix, you can substitute a half cup of unsweetened applesauce for a half cup of butter; a third of a cup of unsweetened cocoa powder for two ounces of baking chocolate; one cup of evaporated skim milk for one cup of heavy cream; and skim milk for whole milk (see Chapter 8 for ingredient substitution ideas). You can also reduce the amount of sugar in a recipe by one-quarter to one-third.

Go easy on the frosting. Most of the sugar and fat lurks in the icing. For example, while a generous slice of yellow cake has about two hundred calories and five grams of fat, the two small tablespoons of vanilla frosting that go on top have about one hundred seventy calories and seven grams of fat. Reduced-fat frostings and fat-free whipped toppings often make tasty alternatives.

Top it off lightly. As an alternative to rich ice cream treats, serve reduced-fat ice cream or frozen yogurt topped with dried fruit such as raisins or cherries, or fresh berries, or nuts.

Watch the portions. There's no need for giant-size servings. Let kids ask for seconds if they want more cake.

IT'S PARTY TIME!

Whether you opt to host a birthday party in your home or at another location like a movie theater or bowling alley, here are two action-packed birthday party ideas and theme cakes that are sure to be a hit with grade-schoolers.

◆   ◆   ◆

Blast-Off-to-the-Moon Rocket Ship Cake

For younger grade-schoolers

makes 10 to 12 servings

red food coloring
1   package of reduced-fat vanilla frosting mix
1   ice cream cone
1   premade jelly roll cake from your bakery
6   rectangular waffle wafer cookies
red or black strands of licorice
assorted round or square candy for details

Add the red food coloring to one-third of the frosting. Cover the ice cream cone with the red frosting, and set aside. Stand the jelly roll upright. (If necessary, trim the bottom end of the jelly roll to make it even.)

Spread the remaining frosting over the jelly roll cake. Add the ice cream cone to the top of the cake. Slice the wafer cookies diagonally, and place them around the bottom of the cake. Decorate the rest of the rocket with the licorice and candy. Dismantle the rocket, and turn the cake on its side before cutting and serving with vanilla frozen yogurt.

◆ ◆ ◆

Party Tips

Rent an inflatable play tent for your guests to bounce around and play in.

Come up with your own variations of popular party games, like pin the planet on the galaxy.

Create an intergalactic space mural by letting everyone draw a picture of their favorite alien.

◆ ◆ ◆

A "Virtual" Party Computer Cake

For older grade-schoolers

makes 16 to 20 servings

4   packages of reduced-fat cake mix
nonstick vegetable spray
4   cans reduced-fat vanilla frosting
1   red or black licorice whip
1   Twinkie
26 pieces of little square candies (like Pez)
several tubes of colored decorator icing

Prepare the cake mix according to package directions. Coat two 13" × 9" × 2" glass baking pans with nonstick spray. Pour batter into each pan, and bake as directed. Remove from the oven.

When the cakes have completely cooled, remove them from the pans. Cut one of the cakes in half. Put the uncut cake on a large platter, and frost the whole cake. Place one of the cake halves at the far end of the larger cake, and frost completely. Stack the remaining cake on top of the cake half, and finish frosting the tops and sides.

Stick one end of the licorice whip into the side of the computer cake and the other end into the Twinkie (your mouse!). Strategically place the square candies on the front of the cake so they look like typewriter keys. With decorator icing, draw a border on the "computer screen," and write a birthday message.

◆　◆　◆

Party Tips

E-mail invitations or send computer-theme invitations to your guests. Follow up with "electronic" thank-you notes.

Select a popular video or computer game as a party theme, and have guests come dressed as their favorite character.

Send guests on a scavenger hunt to look for items that appear in the video or computer game.

SEASON'S EATINGS!

'Tis the season for family, friends, fun, and lots of food. Because certain holidays come only once a year, you can relax the rules a bit when it comes to eating that Halloween booty or Fourth of July apple pie. Here are some tips on how to keep your child's holiday spirits bright and food choices light.

Plan ahead. If your child is going to attend a holiday party with lots of sugary treats, make sure he eats a nutritious meal beforehand. Let him enjoy a few treats at the party, but make sure he brushes and flosses his teeth when he gets home.

Step up physical activity. With so many tempting goodies to eat, make sure your child gets plenty of exercise to help her burn off extra calories. Aim for 60 minutes of physical activity a day (see Chapter 9 for more information about kids and physical activity). This can include dancing at parties, playing outside, roller-skating, or going for nature walks.

Go easy on the soda and fruit drinks. These beverages contain large amounts of added sugar and few nutrients. Instead, offer your child water, low-fat milk, or 100 percent fruit juice to drink during the holiday celebration.

Tips for Dealing with Halloween Candy Overload

Halloween candy can be every parent's nutritional nightmare. Here's how you can tame your little candy-loving monsters:

- *Set trick-or-treating curfews.* Limit the number of hours your child is out trick-or-treating to help cut down on the amount of candy she collects. Serve lunch or dinner before your child goes out, since this will help prevent her from gorging on candy when she gets home.

- *Negotiate how long the candy will remain in the house.* Decide, for instance, that all candy is thrown out after one week. Once the novelty of eating the candy wears off, it often loses its appeal.

- *Keep candy out of sight (and out of mind).* Store the candy in out-of-reach places like high cupboards or the freezer. Chances are your child will forget about it.

- *Get kids moving.* Make sure your child gets a little extra physical activity such as riding a bike or jumping rope, to help compensate for all those Halloween treats.

Stack the "food" deck. Since you already know that your child will have access to several high-fat, sugary treats during the year-end holidays, plan to serve at least one nutritious holiday dish. If you are eating elsewhere, offer to bring the dish along; or better yet, let your child help you decide what to prepare, and let him help you make it.

CELEBRATE GOOD TIMES!

Try celebrating the holidays with these tempting recipes. Each offers your child a lighter alternative to popular holiday fare.

◆ ◆ ◆

Chinese New Year

Chinese Egg Drop Soup
makes 6 servings

2 eggs, beaten
3 14-ounce cans reduced-sodium chicken broth
½ teaspoon garlic powder
¼ teaspoon ground ginger
4 green onions, diced
1 cup frozen peas, thawed

Break the eggs in a small mixing bowl, and beat briskly with a fork. Set aside. Put the chicken broth, garlic powder, and ginger in a saucepan and simmer over medium heat. Bring to just under a boil. While stirring the soup, pour the beaten eggs over the tines of a fork into the soup mixture. (The eggs will cook immediately in feathery wisps.) When the eggs are cooked, immediately toss in the green onions and peas, and serve. For best results, make this soup right before you plan to serve it.

◆ ◆ ◆

◆ ◆ ◆

Cinco de Mayo

Fiesta Quesadillas

makes 4 servings

½ cup shredded reduced-fat Monterey Jack cheese
½ cup shredded reduced-fat cheddar cheese
nonstick spray
8 (8-inch) flour tortillas
¼ cup thinly sliced scallions
1 cup canned Mexican-style corn, drained

Combine the cheeses, and set aside. Coat a baking sheet with nonstick spray. Brush one side of each tortilla lightly with water. Lay 4 of the tortillas, moist side down, on the baking sheet. Spread some of the cheese mixture on each of the 4 tortillas. Top with the scallions and corn. Cover with the remaining tortillas, placing them moist side up.

Bake at 400 degrees F for 10 minutes, or until the quesadillas are heated through and the cheese is melted.

◆ ◆ ◆

Fourth of July

Red, White, and Blue Yogurt Parfaits

makes 4 servings

1 cup red raspberries or sliced strawberries
2 cups vanilla low-fat yogurt
1 cup blueberries

Wash the berries, drain, and remove any stems. Fill the bottom of a parfait dish with a small amount of the raspberries or strawberries. Add some yogurt, and then a few blueberries. Repeat the three layers, ending with the blueberries.

◆　◆　◆

Halloween

Witches' Fingers

makes 4 servings

nonstick spray
4　chicken cutlets
1　cup all-purpose flour
2　egg whites, beaten
1　cup bread crumbs
1　6-ounce can black olives, pitted and drained
2　cups cooked rice

Spray a cookie sheet with the nonstick spray. Slice the cutlets into strips about the width of one finger. (Don't worry about cutting them straight; the more crooked, the better!) Place the flour, beaten egg whites, and bread crumbs in separate bowls, and line the bowls up next to one another. Dust the chicken strips with the flour, dip them into the bowl of egg whites, and roll them in the bread crumbs. Place the strips on the cookie sheet, and broil for about five minutes on each side until golden brown.

To make the witches' fingernails, cut the olives in half lengthwise. Trim the halves into pointy nail shapes, and place on top of the chicken strips. Serve the chicken strips on a bed of rice. "Bone" appetit!

◆　◆　◆

◆　◆　◆

Thanksgiving

Wild Rice and Dried Cranberry Stuffing
makes 8 servings

2　teaspoons canola oil
1　cup celery, chopped
1½ cups onion, chopped
2　tablespoons freshly grated orange peel
1　cup dried cranberries
1　6-ounce box of instant long-grain and wild rice, prepared, or 3 cups of cooked wild rice
nonstick cooking spray

Heat the oil in a nonstick skillet over medium-high heat. When hot, add the celery, onions, orange peel, and dried cranberries, and stir-fry for about four minutes. Add the cooked wild rice, and stir until combined.

Coat a casserole dish with the nonstick cooking spray. Add the rice mixture to the dish, and bake uncovered at 350 degrees F for 40 minutes.

◆　◆　◆

◆ ◆ ◆

Christmas

Veggie Wreath and Snowball Dip

makes 8 servings

Wreath Ingredients

2   heads of broccoli
1   head of cauliflower
9   cherry tomatoes

Dip Ingredients

2   cups fat-free plain yogurt
½ cup reduced-fat mayonnaise
½ envelope of powdered salad dressing (your child's favorite)

To make the wreath, wash the broccoli and cauliflower. Chop the stems off, and cut the florets into bite-size pieces. Wash the cherry tomatoes, and slice in half. Arrange the broccoli florets in a circle on a serving platter. Leave a space in the center of the circle that is large enough for the bowl of dip. Place the cherry tomatoes on top of the broccoli florets in clusters of three so they look like berries. Fill in any background space on the platter with the cauliflower to create the look of snow.

To make the dip, stir the yogurt, mayonnaise, and salad dressing mix together; cover with plastic wrap and refrigerate until you're ready to use. Spoon the dip into a serving bowl, and place the bowl in the center of the wreath.

◆ ◆ ◆

◆ ◆ ◆

Kwanza

Pineapple Upside-Down Cakes

makes 24 cupcakes

½ cup margarine
1 large can pineapple tidbits, packed in natural juice
1 package reduced-fat yellow cake
1½ cups brown sugar
24 maraschino cherries

Preheat oven to 350 degrees F. Melt the margarine in a saucepan, and pour a small amount in each muffin tin (just enough to cover the bottom of the tin). Drain the pineapple, and set aside the juice. Prepare the cake mix according to package directions, but use the pineapple juice instead of water.

Add one tablespoon of brown sugar and about six pineapple tidbits to each muffin tin. Pour the cake batter into each tin and fill until the batter is level with the top of the tin. Bake according to package directions. Cool about five minutes on a wire rack; then remove the cupcakes from the tins. If any of the brown sugar–pineapple mixture sticks to the muffin tins, scoop it out and add it back to the cupcake. Top each upside-down cake with a cherry.

◆ ◆ ◆

◆ ◆ ◆

Hanukkah

Potato Pancakes (Latkes)

makes 4 pancakes

3 medium potatoes
½ small onion
2 egg whites, slightly beaten
¼ cup flour
¼ teaspoon pepper
½ teaspoon salt
¼ teaspoon baking powder
nonstick spray

Preheat the oven to 425 degrees F. Boil the potatoes until tender. Let cool. Peel and grate the potatoes and onions. Stir the egg whites and remaining ingredients into the potato-and-onion mixture. Form into pancakes and place on a cookie sheet that has been sprayed with the nonstick spray. Bake 10 to 12 minutes. Flip the pancakes, and bake an additional 10 to 12 minutes until crispy. Note: Rather than cooking, peeling, and grating your own potatoes, you can save time by buying precooked, frozen shredded hash browns.

◆ ◆ ◆

EXTRA-CREDIT ASSIGNMENT

Your Order, Please?

Ask your child to select one of her favorite extracurricular eating spots, and have her try to select a healthy meal from the menu items offered. Then together, evaluate her choices using the Five-Star Criteria listed in the following chapters:

Breakfast—Chapter 3

Lunch—Chapter 4

Dinner—Chapter 5

Snacks—Chapter 6

CHAPTER 8

Culinary Kids

◆ ◆ ◆

Are we having chicken and broccoli again for dinner?
—JORDAN, SIXTH GRADE

You never buy the cereal I like.
—NICOLETTE, FOURTH GRADE

Why do I have to wash my hands before setting the table?
—MAURA, SECOND GRADE

**Top Three Mistakes Parents Make
When Cooking with Their Kids:**

1. Never take the time to plan menus.
2. Don't let them help with the cooking.
3. Not sure how to read food labels.

Grade-schoolers love to experiment *and* create things! They also want to be included in family decisions, especially the ones that involve them. So why not take advantage of these qualities right in your own kitchen? There's no better way to get your child to try a new food than by letting him pick it out in the supermarket and help prepare it at home. Planning menus, comparing food labels, shopping for food, and cooking are important ways your child can begin to discover the delicious world of healthy eating. In this chapter, you'll:

- explore ways to get your grade-schooler interested in food from planning healthy menus to developing important cooking skills;
- discover strategies to help you and your child become savvy food shoppers;
- learn important facts about food safety.

THE PRINCIPLES OF MENU PLANNING

It's four in the afternoon, and you've been so busy all day that you haven't given dinner a moment's thought. So you end up opening a box of Hamburger Helper or packing the kids in the car to grab some fast food. You tell yourself that things will be different next week; you're going to *plan* meals in advance. Sound familiar? Well, here's your chance to learn how to keep that promise.

A Little Planning Goes a Long Way

Although it may seem hard to believe, the fifteen or twenty minutes you spend planning meals for the week actually save you hours of time. That's because a little advance planning will help prevent those time-consuming last-minute trips to the grocery store or fast-food restaurants. In addition, planning meals can:

- *get your grade-schooler excited about eating healthy foods.* If you let your child help select what you're going to serve, chances are good that he'll be much more likely to eat it.
- *increase the variety in your family's diet.* Being better prepared means you'll be more likely to try new foods and new cooking methods.

- *save you money.* If you know what foods you'll need for the week, you can look for coupons or store specials. You can also use what you have at home before it spoils, or take advantage of leftovers.

Making Menus

The best way to plan meals ahead of time is to make a weekly menu. Once your menu is planned, you can write a grocery list, estimate how much preparation is needed, and decide what you can make ahead of time. The following tips will make your meals easier to prepare and more nutritious.

Organize your recipes.   This may be time-consuming at first, but once you've completed this step you'll reap the rewards. Use whatever system works best for you, such as putting recipes in alphabetical order or organizing them by ingredient. Let your grade-schooler get involved by creating a recipe box or placing stickers on her favorite recipes.

Develop a menu-planning routine.   Set a time once a week to sit down with your child to write up a menu. Pick a time that works best, like Sunday night after dinner. Before you begin, check your calendar to see if there are any special events during the week like a band concert or school meeting. If you know it's going to be a hectic week, include lots of easy-to-prepare items or meals that you can make ahead of time.

Build menus with "pyramid" power.   Use the Food Guide Pyramid (see Chapter 2) to plan each of your meals. That way you're sure to meet everyone's daily food-group requirements. Remember to use the Five-Star Criteria for planning breakfast (Chapter 3), lunch (Chapter 4), dinner (Chapter 5), and snacks (Chapter 6).

Get everyone involved.   Have each family member plan a night or two of meals, *or* have them select one item for the meal. Encourage your child to look for new recipes in cookbooks, magazines, or on the Internet, and then designate one night each week to experiment. At the end of the month, decide which recipe (or recipes) you preferred.

LABEL-READING LITERACY

Before you and your grade-schooler use your menu-planning tactics to hit the supermarket, it helps to know some of the basics of label reading. That's because food labels provide a wealth of information that can help you choose foods that are good sources of nutrients such as fiber, calcium, and iron, *and* help limit the fat, cholesterol, and sodium in your child's diet.

Labels at a Glance

If you're not sure what to look for, label reading may take a few extra minutes. But once you're familiar with the words and numbers, you'll be reading labels in just a flash. Constance Geiger, Ph.D., R.D., a renowned expert on food labels and an assistant professor of food and nutrition at the University of Utah in Salt Lake City offers the following strategies to help you get out of the grocery store in record time with a cartload of tasty, healthy foods.

The Label-Reading Shortcut Method. For those days when you're short on time, glance at the *front* of the package and look for claims. Thanks to the 1994 Nutrition Labeling and Education Act, each of the nutrient claims, like "low-fat" or "healthy," now has a uniform definition for each type of food it appears on (see sidebar "A Dictionary of Nutrient Claims"). For example, if you buy low-fat hot dogs, low-fat cookies, or low-fat yogurt, each of these foods must contain no more than three grams of fat per serving in order to claim that they are low in fat.

You can also check for health-related claims such as "Oatmeal Helps Reduce Cholesterol." Manufacturers can *only* make these claims on their packages if there is a great deal of evidence supporting them, and if they've been approved by the FDA.

Finally, certain beverages, like juices and fruit drinks, must state on the front of the label the actual percentage of fruit juice that's in the product. So if you were trying to decide between two fruit drinks, your healthier buy would be the beverage with the higher percentage of fruit juice.

A Dictionary of Nutrition Claims

On the front of most packages, you'll find a variety of claims ranging from "fat free" to "healthy." Here's a quick overview of what the terms really mean. (For more specifics about nutrient claims and label reading visit the FDA Web site at www.FDA.gov.)

Free: contains no fat, or insignificant amounts of fat, saturated fat, cholesterol, sodium, sugar, or calories per serving.

Low Fat: contains three grams or less per serving.

Low Saturated Fat: contains one gram or less per serving.

Low Cholesterol: contains twenty milligrams or less of cholesterol and two grams or less of saturated fat per serving.

Low Calorie: contains forty calories or less per serving.

Reduced: contains at least twenty-five percent less of a nutrient (such as fat, cholesterol, sodium, or calories) than the regular product.

Light: the food must contain one-third fewer calories or half the fat of the regular product, or the sodium content of a low-calorie, low-fat food has been reduced by at least fifty percent.

The Label-Reading Comparison Method.   When you're trying to decide which product to buy, read the Nutrition Facts on the *back* of the package. The Nutrition Facts Panel is jam-packed with excellent nutrition information. But let's face it, most of us are not mathematicians, and we don't have time to analyze the label in depth. The

Nutrition Facts

Serving Size ½ cup (114g)
Servings Per Container 4

Amount Per Serving

Calories 90   Calories from Fat 30

	% Daily Value*
Total Fat 3g	5%
Saturated Fat 0g	0%
Cholesterol 0mg	0%
Sodium 300mg	13%
Total Carbohydrate 13g	4%
Dietary Fiber 3g	12%
Sugars 3g	
Protein 3g	

Vitamin A 80%	*	Vitamin C 60%
Calcium 4%	*	Iron 4%

*Percent Daily Values are based on a 2,000 calorie diet. Your daily values may be higher or lower depending on your calorie needs.

	Calories	2,000	2,500
Total Fat	Less than	55g	80g
Sat Fat	Less than	20g	25g
Cholesterol	Less than	300mg	300mg
Sodium	Less than	2,400mg	2,400mg
Total Carbohydrate		300g	375g
Dietary		25g	30g

Calories per gram
Fat 9 • Carbohydrate 4 • Protein 4

A typical nutrition label.

good news is that it's not necessary to understand everything. The key is to focus on the specific areas that you are most concerned about. For instance:

Size up the serving. Because all of the nutrition information on a food label is based on the serving size that's listed, be sure to compare it to your child's actual serving size. Kids often eat smaller portions, so you may need to make some adjustments. For example, if a serving of milk is listed as one cup, and your child drinks only half a cup, divide the nutrition information in half.

Check out the calories. Make sure your child is getting one or more nutrients along with those calories. Important nutrients for kids include protein to help your child grow; calcium for strong bones and teeth; iron for healthy blood; vitamin A for better vision; and vitamin C to help heal cuts and scrapes (see Appendix A for more information about nutrients and their functions).

Shy away from sugar. Sugar provides calories but few, if any, nutrients for your child. Plus eating too much sugar (and other carbohydrates) has been linked to dental cavities. Remember that every four grams of sugar listed on the food label equals one teaspoon of sugar. So if your child's favorite cereal has sixteen grams of sugar per one-cup serving, that would amount to a whopping four teaspoons of sugar! And if he normally eats two cups of cereal, that would total up to eight teaspoons of sugar!

Focus on dietary fiber. Encourage your child to eat foods with dietary fiber like whole-grain breads and cereals. Foods with dietary fiber can help prevent your child from being constipated and possibly ward off future diseases like cancer and heart disease. How much dietary fiber does your child need? As mentioned before, a good rule of thumb is to add five grams of fiber to his age. For example, if your son is seven years old, he should eat about twelve grams of fiber a day (for more information on fiber see Chapter 2).

Find out about fat. The total amount of fat and saturated fat will always appear on the food label. Limiting fat in a child's diet helps prevent future health problems such as heart disease and certain types of cancer. When selecting products, always compare the fat content and purchase the one with the lowest amount.

Use the Percent Daily Values (% DV). The % DV is a useful piece of information on the label that can help you determine whether the nutrients in a serving of food contribute a lot or a little to your child's total daily diet. (By *diet* we mean all the different foods your child eats in a day.) A high percentage, 20 percent or greater, means the food has a *lot* of a certain nutrient, which is what you'll want to look for with nutrients like dietary fiber, vitamins, and minerals. A low percentage, 5 percent or less, means the food has only a little of that nutrient, which is what you'll want to see for fat, saturated fat, cholesterol, and sodium.

Scan the ingredient list for specific information. The ingredient list tells you exactly what's in a food. This can be helpful if you are trying to stay away from certain ingredients because of health reasons or if your child has an allergy. For example, if your child has a milk allergy, you would want to avoid foods that contain casein or whey, which are forms of milk protein. Also, keep in mind that ingredients are listed by weight from most to least. Those listed first are the main ingredients.

Teaching Your Child Label-Reading Basics

If you want your child to eat smart, one of the most important skills you can teach him is how to read food labels. Most kids are ready to learn how to read labels by around age six. Here are some ways to help your child start making sense of food labels.

Go on a scavenger hunt. Give your child a list of items to find in the grocery store such as fat-free ice cream or low-sodium soup, and ask her to select these foods by searching for claims on the *front* of the package.

Compare serving sizes. At home, have your child locate the serving size on the Nutrition Facts Panel of some of her favorite foods like apple juice, pretzels, and cereal. Take out your measuring cups and spoons, and let her measure the serving size. Then ask her to compare her usual portion to the serving size listed on the food label to see if there is a difference.

Practice math homework. Have your child determine how much sugar is in his favorite cereal, then divide the number of grams by four to find out how many teaspoons of sugar it has.

SUPERMARKET SAVVY

Now that you've achieved label literacy, it's time to sharpen your shopping skills. (And with more than thirty thousand products to choose from, let's face it—it's a jungle out there!) If you're looking for ways to save time and a few dollars, here are some quick supermarket-survival strategies.

Make a list—and stick to it. Making a list will actually save you time at the grocery store. It will help jog your memory and eliminate those Darn-I-forgot-to-buy-it trips to the store. Plus, it will keep you focused and decrease the likelihood of impulse buying.

Do your shopping at off-hours. If possible, beat crowds by shopping early in the morning, late at night, or during the week, rather than on the weekends.

Always eat before you go shopping. Those free samples at the grocery store can be very tempting, but if you're full, chances are you'll be able to resist them. Being full can also curb your appetite for buying items that are not on your list.

Shop the perimeter of the store. All the major food groups can be found around the outer rim of the store at the bake shop, deli counter, produce department, and dairy section. Stay away from the aisle-by-aisle shopping, and you'll trim some time off your shopping trip.

Put your older child to work. Give him a section of your grocery list, and let him go on a scavenger hunt for these items. And when you get home, a second set of hands makes unloading the car a lot easier.

Beware of the checkout lines. Those candy bars and special promotion items are there for a reason. As you're waiting in line, it's hard to resist them, especially with your son or daughter begging you to buy something.

Try grocery shopping on-line. If shopping on the Internet appeals to you, check out home-delivery services in your area. You can shop at whatever time is convenient for you and avoid supermarket distractions.

Should I Buy Organic Produce?

The answer to this question is really a personal one. The truth of the matter is that *all* fruits and vegetables are safe for your child to eat. While conventionally grown fruits and vegetables may contain pesticide residues, they only contain minuscule amounts of them. That's because the Environmental Protections Agency and the Food and Drug Administration have worked together to establish national pesticide regulations. If you buy conventionally grown produce, you can reduce the threat of any pesticides by:

- washing fruits and vegetables with warm water to remove dirt and other residues from the surface.
- removing the outer leaves of leafy vegetables like lettuce and cabbage.
- giving your child a variety of fruits and vegetables so that you minimize her repeated exposure to the same pesticides.

If you do opt to buy organic produce, you'll find the recent labeling requirements for organic foods helpful. According to the new standards, organic products are now divided into four categories:

1. Products labeled "100 percent organic" must consist solely of organic ingredients.
2. Products labeled "organic" must contain at least 95 percent organic ingredients.
3. Products labeled "made with organic ingredients" must consist of at least 70 percent organic ingredients.
4. Products containing less than 70 percent organic ingredients are not allowed to place the word "organic" anywhere on the front of the package, but may list specific organic ingredients in the ingredient list.

THE JOY OF COOKING WITH KIDS

Understanding the basics of menu planning and label reading will help your child learn more about *selecting* healthy foods. The next step involves teaching her about *preparing* foods so that she learns to enjoy eating them. Although cooking with kids can get messy, it's worth it. Children need to learn about cooking at an early age because it's a skill that will serve them well for a lifetime. Home-prepared foods have the potential to be your healthiest option because you're in control; you can select the freshest ingredients, leave the teaspoon of salt out of the pasta water, or cook your food with little or no added fat. Just think of your kitchen as a classroom in disguise, because food preparation can be a springboard for learning. Teaching your child to cook can:

entice him to try new foods. Kids are much more willing to eat foods like meat loaf or tuna casserole if they have helped to prepare them.

bolster self-esteem. Children are proud of what they make and receive immediate gratification once they've started their creation.

improve language skills. Kids will need to read recipes and recall the order of directions. And they will build their vocabulary as they become familiar with new words like *sauté*, *mince*, and *knead*.

enhance math skills. When following recipes that call for ¼ teaspoon of baking soda or ¾ cup of water, older children can apply their knowledge of fractions and units of measure; younger children can measure flour or sugar with spoons and cups.

turn her on to the sciences. Kids can learn about the principles of cause and effect as you explain such concepts as how a liquid (juice) turns into a solid (Popsicle®).

improve large- and small-motor skills. Whenever kids are rolling, stirring, kneading, or peeling, they are exercising the muscles in their hands and arms and improving dexterity.

promote future health. If children learn about nutrition and how to prepare foods in tasty ways, they may end up eating more healthfully throughout their lives.

Playing It Safe

Before your child actually "gets cooking," you'll need to teach him some kitchen and food-handling safety rules. Here are a few ground rules to review each time you're together in the kitchen.

1. To prevent germs from getting on food or cooking utensils, make sure hands are washed with warm, soapy water and long hair is pulled back.
2. Older kids (ages nine and up) need to pay careful attention when they are chopping with knives or using a grater. And always show your child how to safely use kitchen equipment, like mixers, food processors, and blenders.
3. Keep pot holders close to the oven, microwave, or stove. To prevent kids from touching or bumping into hot pots and pans, always use the back burners of your stove. If front burners must be used, turn pot handles toward the back of the stove.
4. Never eat raw ingredients. Batter with raw eggs could pose a hazard for salmonella, a bacterial infection that gets into the gastrointestinal tract and causes vomiting and diarrhea.

Frequently Asked Questions about Washing Hands

So often we tell our children "Wash your hands!" But do they really know *why* we want them to do it, and *how* to wash them correctly? Here are the answers to some tough questions about hand washing.

Q: *How often should I wash my hands?*
A: You should always wash your hands in warm, soapy water before handling and preparing raw meat, poultry, or

seafood. It's also important to wash hands *after* certain tasks such as handling raw meat and then cutting vegetables, and after taking out garbage, sneezing, or petting your dog or cat.

Q: *How long do I need to wash my hands in order to remove germs?*

A: Sing two choruses of "Happy Birthday" while you lather your hands for twenty seconds. Always wash both the front and back of your hands all the way up to your wrists, and don't forget to scrub between fingers and under fingernails. Dry your hands with disposable paper towels or clean towels.

Q: *Are antibacterial products more effective in killing germs than plain soap and water?*

A: Washing your hands for twenty seconds with any type of soap and warm water is effective in reducing bacteria. There is no scientific evidence that proves antibacterial soap is more effective in reducing the incidence of disease than plain soap.

Source: *Home Food Safety . . . It's in Your Hands*™, The American Dietetic Association and Its Foundation, and the ConAgra Foundation.

Ready, Set, Cook

Even if you're not a gourmet chef, there's no need to fret. Cooking with your child *can* be a positive experience for both of you, regardless of your cooking expertise. When teaching your child to cook, brush off your old Home Economics 101 notes. Then start with the basics, such as reading a recipe or mastering a simple task like cracking an egg. Here are some important cooking skills that you'll want to teach your child.

Follow the recipe. Take a few recipes and go through each step with your child. By age five your child should be able to help you start reading a recipe, and by age nine, she should be able to follow a recipe on her own. Be sure to have her check out the ingredient list and needed equipment before she begins cooking.

Measure it up. The secret to successful cooking is measuring correctly. Discuss the importance of accurate measuring and the different types of utensils you'll need to use. For example, see-through measuring cups are best suited for measuring liquids such as milk or water, because you can see the markings more clearly. Dry ingredients can be measured with metal or plastic cups. Use measuring spoons when only a small amount of an ingredient is needed.

Master the cooking methods. Start with easy cooking techniques like mixing or rolling. As you try different recipes, explain what methods are called for and their purpose. For example, discuss the difference between beating and mixing or baking and broiling. If you're not sure, you'll find this information in the glossary of most cookbooks.

Look Who's Cooking!

The trick to cooking with kids is matching their cooking skills with their age and developmental abilities. These general guidelines can help you determine what types of cooking experiences you should try with your child. Be sure to provide close supervision when cooking with kids, and remind them of the importance of washing their hands and other safety precautions, like never touching a hot stove or cutting properly with a sharp knife.

Five- and six-year-olds (with minimal assistance) can:

sort food items by shape and color
stir cool mixtures like instant pudding
tear lettuce

snap green beans
pour milk from a small pitcher

Seven- and eight-year-olds can:

shuck corn
roll with a rolling pin
mix and shake
spread peanut butter with a dull knife or spreader
measure ingredients
rinse vegetables
toast bread in a toaster
crack an egg

Nine- and ten-year-olds can:

knead bread dough
cut with a table knife
grate cheese
stir hot mixtures
broil with a toaster oven
blend foods in a blender

Grade-schoolers age ten and older can:

slice or chop (carefully!) with a sharp knife
bake or broil using the oven
boil, poach, or simmer using the stove
microwave popcorn and other prepackaged items

Ingredient-Substitution Chart

When cooking or baking with your child, teach her how to make some of these healthy substitutions. They won't alter the taste, but they will trim calories and fat grams tremendously.

Instead of:	Try:
1 cup chopped almonds	½ cup chopped almonds and ½ cup crisp rice cereal
½ cup butter or oil (for baking)	½ cup unsweetened applesauce or ½ cup baby-food pureed prunes
2 ounces baking chocolate	⅓ cup unsweetened cocoa powder
1 cup chocolate chips	½ cup mini chocolate chips
1 whole egg	2 egg whites
1 cup heavy cream	1 cup evaporated skim milk
1 cup sour cream	1 cup nonfat plain yogurt
1 cup whipped cream	1 cup nondairy light whipped topping
1 cup whole milk	1 cup fat-free milk

KID-FRIENDLY KITCHEN CONCOCTIONS

Your child will have a blast whipping up these tasty recipes. Most ten-year-olds should be able to prepare any of them on their own. Younger grade-schoolers can make them, too, but will require some assistance. Just be sure to assign them tasks that are appropriate for their age and skill level.

◆ ◆ ◆

Frozen Fruit Cones

makes 4 servings

⅔   cup fresh strawberries
¼   cup sugar
1⅓ cups nonfat plain yogurt
4   ice cream cones

Place the strawberries, sugar, and yogurt in a blender. Cover, and blend until smooth. Pour the mixture into a baking pan, and cover with plastic wrap. Freeze for at least 12 hours. Scoop the frozen yogurt into the ice cream cones, and serve.

◆ ◆ ◆

Super-Easy Nacho Bites

makes 1 serving

6 large baked tortilla chips
2 tablespoons fat-free refried beans
2 tablespoons chunky salsa
¼ cup shredded reduced-fat cheddar cheese

Arrange the chips in a single layer on a microwave-safe plate. Spoon the beans onto the chips, top them with the salsa and sprinkle with cheese. Microwave the nacho bites at medium (50 percent) power for one minute then rotate the dish. Continue to microwave for another 30 to 60 seconds, or until the cheese is melted.

EXTRA-CREDIT ASSIGNMENT

Hunting for the Healthiest Buys!

After teaching your kids how to read food labels, take them grocery shopping and have them search for the healthiest buys. Set
up the activity like a scavenger hunt. Here are some options:

1. Have children look for three products that have less than
   three grams of fat.
2. Select one specific product like frozen pizza or canned
   ravioli. Ask your children to find the brand that is the lowest in fat and/or provides the most vitamins and minerals.
3. Challenge your kids to read food labels and find three
   items that will make a nutritious and fast dinner.
4. Ask them to find one food item from your shopping list
   from each of the five food groups.

CHAPTER 9

Physical Activity

A Moving Subject

◆ ◆ ◆

Can I have some friends over to play video games?
— JACK, FIRST GRADE

I'll go outside when my TV show is over.
— DANIELLE, FIFTH GRADE

Playing baseball isn't fun anymore.
— COLIN, FOURTH GRADE

**Top Three Mistakes Parents Make with
Their Children Regarding Physical Activity:**

1. Not physically active themselves.
2. Let kids spend too much time watching TV or playing on the computer.
3. Not sure which sports are best for their kids.

Does your child spend more time watching TV or playing video games than riding his bike, playing tag, or shooting hoops with friends? If you answered yes, you're not alone. Less than 25 percent of grade school children get the recommended sixty minutes of physical activity each day. Even more alarming, physical activity declines dramatically as children enter the middle and high school years. That's why it's so important to get your grade-schooler hooked on physical activity. In this chapter you'll:

- find out how much physical activity your child needs each day to reap the benefits of being fit;
- discover strategies to help motivate your child to turn off the TV or computer and start moving;
- learn how to keep your child fueled for fitness and fun.

COUCH POTATOES BREED TATER TOTS

There are many reasons why kids today are less active than ever before. For one thing, they spend less time in gym class at school, and their free time is filled with "electronic" entertainment, such as video games, television, and the Internet. Kids also are less likely to walk to school or to a friend's house; and, most important, *many parents are physically inactive.* Studies have repeatedly shown that parents who model and support an active lifestyle in their children typically have the most physically active kids. In other words, if you're a couch potato, chances are good that your child will be one, too. The Surgeon General's Report on Physical Activity revealed that active children are more likely to have parents who:

- engage in physical activities or play sports with them;
- watch them take part in physical activities or organized sports;
- take them to physical activities or organized sports;
- feel it's important for them to participate in physical activities or organized sports

If you want to teach your grade-schooler how to be physically active, you need to make fitness a family affair. Throughout this chapter, we will provide you with suggestions on how to teach your child to make fitness a priority.

Getting Your School More Involved in Physical Education

With all the academic requirements facing school administration, physical education (PE) often gets pushed to the bottom of the priority list. Less time and money is being spent on developing quality PE programs in many schools. Here are some strategies you can use to make PE a priority in your child's school.

- Write to and speak with school administrators to express your support for quality PE programs.
- Encourage school officials to provide opportunities for students to be active before and after school. For example, offering after-school sports intramurals like flag football is a great way for kids to stay active.
- Encourage your school to coordinate family evenings and weekend activities like sports nights.
- Get your local parent-teacher association to sponsor physical activities like "fun runs" or "dance-a-thons."

The Benefits of Moving Each Day

Numerous studies in recent years have discussed the benefits of regular physical activity in adults. Physical activity that is performed daily can help reduce the risk of developing diabetes, heart disease, high blood pressure, and colon cancer. In addition, regular physical activity can help adults maintain a healthy weight and reduce depression and anxiety. Research has also shown that the benefits of regular physical activity can have a positive influence on the health and well-being of children. According to the Center for Disease Control and Prevention, regular physical activity in childhood and adolescence:

- improves strength, flexibility, and endurance
- helps build and maintain healthy bones and muscles
- helps control weight and reduce fat
- reduces anxiety and stress
- increases self-esteem
- may reduce blood pressure and cholesterol levels.

In addition, young people say they like physical activity because it's fun, and they can do it with friends, and it helps them learn skills, stay in shape, and look better.

The Grade School Years: A Golden Opportunity

The grade school years are the most important time in your child's life to teach physical fitness. In the early grade school years (ages five through eight), kids move around just to have fun. In the later grade school years (ages nine through twelve), kids start to participate in sports. Competition, and a strong emphasis on winning, begin to place unwanted pressure on many kids. According to fitness expert Kenneth Cooper, M.D., in his book *Fit Kids*, the most serious threat to physical activity begins as early as age nine. Many children feel that they're not good enough to play sports or they don't react well to competition. As a result, they drop out of organized sports programs and sometimes are turned off to any type of physical activity.

Parents play a crucial role in providing support and encouragement during the grade school years. Your job is to help your child find physical activities he enjoys and feels comfortable participating in. It's also important to look at your child's level of physical development and understand which activities are appropriate for his age. Most important, you'll want to start putting your child in charge of planning his own activities. We discussed in the introduction how the grade school years were such an important time to shift some of the responsibility of healthy eating off your shoulders and onto your son's or daughter's. This applies to physical activity as well. By high school, it may be too late.

Which Activities Are Right for My Child?

In his book *Fit Kids*, Dr. Cooper outlines activities that are appropriate for the following stages of your child's development. He cautions, though, that parents should always remember that every child is an individual—some kids are able to do things earlier, while some do them later.

Ages Five to Eight: Being Active Just for the Heck of It. Children in this age group run, jump, and play sports because it seems like the natural thing to do. They just want to play and really don't care much about winning. They want to have fun, be with friends, and burn off energy. They are now able to integrate physical and cognitive skills; for example, after catching a ball they will spontaneously throw it back. Your job at this phase is to make sure that your child has adequate time and space to be as active as possible. You should also be careful of accidents, as younger children try to test physical boundaries and exert their growing independence.

Ages Eight to Ten: Being Part of a Team. During this time, children discover team sports like soccer, basketball, and baseball. They have developed enough physical skills to make a basket or hit the baseball and can follow the rules. They enjoy being a team player, but still want to have fun. Your job at this phase is to help your child enjoy a variety of activities with friends. Physical development varies greatly among eight- to ten-year-olds, so help *your* child find the activities that she is physically, mentally, and socially ready to handle. Also, be sure to stress activity over competition. This will help to avoid negative experiences, because kids who drop out of sports now may never come back.

Ages Ten to Twelve: The Start of Puberty. Many children will begin going through puberty at around age ten; others may not begin until they're fourteen. This can be a difficult time for many kids.

Some boys develop at a slower rate than their peers and are suddenly at a physical disadvantage. On the other hand, girls' coordination and self-esteem may be affected as they grow taller and start to put on body fat. Your job is to make sure your child is playing sports with others who are at the same stage of physical and social development. Sometimes activities that focus on individual development, like bicycling or hiking, are better. You should also continue to encourage a variety of activities like swimming and skating.

LET'S GET PHYSICAL: HOW MUCH PHYSICAL ACTIVITY DOES MY CHILD NEED?

All kids need daily physical activity. The most recent Dietary Guidelines, which came out in 2000, recommend that kids get at least sixty minutes of moderate to vigorous physical activity a day, which can include jumping, running, swimming, or playing soccer (see Chapter 2). Previous guidelines encouraged people of all ages to participate in at least thirty minutes of physical activity a day. But because of the rapid increase in childhood and adolescent obesity, and an overall decline in the level of children's physical activity, health specialists have doubled the daily "fitness quota" for kids. Experts also recommend that, at least twice a week, children engage in activities like jumping rope and running, which enhance and maintain muscular strength, flexibility, and bone health.

Walk Like an Egyptian: The Kid's Activity Pyramid

In 1996, Park Nicollett Institute, a Minneapolis-based organization that develops community health-education materials and programs, came out with the Kid's Activity Pyramid. Creator Jane Norstrom, an exercise physiologist, developed the pyramid in order to help parents and teachers encourage kids to become more physically active.

Conceptually, the Kid's Activity Pyramid works much like the Food Guide Pyramid (see Chapter 2). Children should try to do

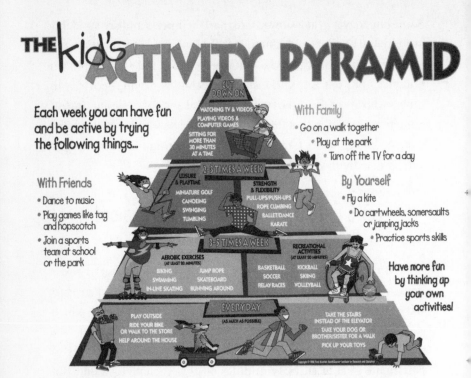

The Kid's Activity Pyramid. *Copyright© 1998 Park Nicollett HealthSource® Park Nicollett Institute. Reprinted by permission.*

more of the physical activities from the bottom of the pyramid and fewer activities from the top. And just as the Food Guide Pyramid recommends, kids need to have a balance as well as a variety of each type of physical activity. Here's how it works.

1. Everyday activities, like playing outside, riding a bike, or helping around the house, are the ones that children should do as much as possible. These types of activities promote getting up and moving rather than sitting.

2. Aerobic exercises like swimming, jumping rope, and in-line skating, and recreational activities, like kickball and soccer, should be performed at least three to five times a week. These types of activities promote cardiovascular fitness.

3. Leisure and playtime activities like swinging and tumbling, and strength and flexibility activities like karate and ballet, focus on strength conditioning and ideally should be performed at least two to three times a week.

4. Sedentary activities, like watching TV, playing video games, or playing on the computer, appear at the tip of the pyramid. Kids should try to cut back on these activities, because they focus on sitting rather than moving.

Norstrom also has several suggestions on how you can help your child put the Kid's Activity Pyramid into motion.

Be a role model. If you want your child to be physically active, he needs to see you walking or playing tennis on a regular basis.

Make sure it's fun. Let your child decide which activities she wants to play. And make sure that if she joins a team, the emphasis is on fun rather than winning.

Turn off the TV and the computer. Watching TV, playing video games, or playing on the computer are fine every once in a while, but they require very little physical activity.

Grab your mitt. Chances are if you offer to play with your child, he'll be more interested in being physically active.

Blast off in backyards and parks. Physical activity doesn't have to come in the form of an organized sport. A neighborhood game of hide-and-seek, for instance, is a fun, action-oriented option for kids.

Sweat the small stuff. When it comes to physical activity, little things do add up. Your child doesn't have to get the recommended amount of daily activity all at once. It can accumulate over the course of the day; for instance, by walking the dog (ten minutes), playing tag at recess (twenty minutes), bike riding (fifteen minutes), and cleaning his room (fifteen minutes), your child can get the recommended sixty minutes of fitness.

Take Control and *Seize* the Remote

Recent studies report that the average child watches between twenty-one and twenty-three hours of television a week. Unfortunately, studies have also shown that the more time children spend in front of the television, the more they are at risk for gaining weight and body fat. What's more, a 1998 study by researchers at San Diego State University found that as parents' and children's TV viewing time went up, performance on a test of aerobic fitness went down.

The American Academy of Pediatrics encourages parents to take control and limit their children's TV time. They provide the following suggestions to keep kid's viewing in balance:

- *Set limits on the amount of TV your child watches.* Aim for no more than one to two hours of quality programming a day. And help your child find other things to do such as playing sports or engaging in hobbies and family activities.
- *Help your child plan TV-viewing time in advance.* At the beginning of each week, have your child choose the programs he wants to watch from among TV listings. Keep copies of the family viewing schedule where everyone can see them.
- *Know what shows your child watches.* Watch TV with your child. If programs show sex, violence, or substance abuse, talk about what you see. This is a good time to reinforce your own family values.
- *Do not permit TV viewing during dinner.* Dinner is often the only time when families are able to be together during the day (see Chapter 5).
- *Keep the TV out of your child's bedroom.* Children not only tend to watch more TV when a set is in their bedroom but

they will probably also spend more time in their room and away from other family members.

- *Set a good example.* If you want your child to go outside instead of watching TV, take a walk or go for a bike ride with her.

FUELING YOUR GRADE-SCHOOLER FOR FITNESS

Whether your child plays quarterback on the football team or in-line skates every day after school with friends, a balanced diet and plenty of fluids can help him stay in the play. This can be a challenge, especially if your child is involved in more than one sport or after-school activity, such as Scouts or music lessons. Kids who are in school all day and then run from one activity to another often hit the playing field dehydrated and hungry. And practices that run well into the evening leave little time for kids to sit down for a family dinner. Taking a time-out for good nutrition is one way you can help your child stay physically active.

Energizing the Young Athlete

Most active grade-schoolers will get the nutrients and energy they need by following the recommendations in the Dietary Guidelines and eating the number of servings recommended in the Food Guide Pyramid (see Chapter 2). Your grade-schooler may need more calories if she is involved in sports. In fact, depending on the frequency, intensity, and duration of the activity, she may need an additional five hundred to one thousand calories a day. Soccer and basketball are examples of high-endurance sports that will burn up a large number of calories. Increasing servings from all of the food groups, especially the grain group, can supply your child with the extra calories and energy she needs. The best way to tell if your child is getting enough calories is to weigh her weekly. You should also watch how well she is performing and ask whether she is "out of steam." Talk with your pediatrician, or dietitian, if you feel your child is not eating enough or gaining enough weight.

Carbs Help Fuel Your Child's Engine

Carbohydrates, the foundation of the Food Guide Pyramid, are the primary fuel for the body. Young athletes depend on generous amounts of carbohydrates for energy during practice and competition. Active children get about half of their total calories from carbohydrates. Since there are four calories per gram of carbohydrates, an active grade-schooler, who needs 2,500 calories per day, would need to eat at least 313 to 343 grams of carbohydrates a day. Here are some examples of carbohydrate-rich foods.

Winning Carbohydrates

	Serving	Grams of Carbohydrate
Apple	1	21
Bagel	½	18
Banana	1	27
Bread	1 slice	12
Cereal	1 cup	24
Corn	½ cup	21
Grapes	½ cup	8
Milk	1 cup	12
Noodles	½ cup (cooked)	20
Pancakes	1	11
Potato	1 large	50
Pretzels	1 ounce	22
Tortilla	1	13

Source: Nutrient data from the Food Processor 7.7 edition, ESHA Research, 2001.

Plan for Snacks

Snacks play an important role in the diet of active kids. For example, Mary's son, Kevin, eats lunch at 11:30 A.M., goes to guitar lessons straight from school, and then heads to baseball practice until 6:00 P.M. A nutritious after-school snack of a banana, yogurt, low-fat granola bar, and plenty of water provides him with the extra energy he needs until his next meal. Snacks also play a key role in fueling kids at all-day sporting tournaments and events. Check out the following chart for nutritious snack ideas that can help propel your grade school athlete toward the finish line. (For more on snacks, see Chapter 6.)

Snacks to Pack for Children

Crunchy	Chewy	Creamy	Juicy
pretzels	raisins	pudding	juice boxes
popcorn	dried fruit	cheese cubes	Jell-O
mini flavored rice cakes	bagels	milk	applesauce
animal crackers	breakfast bars	yogurt	canned fruit
trail mix	rice krispie treats	peanut butter	cherry tomatoes
granola bars	graham crackers	banana	tangerines
baked chips	chewy granola bars		oranges
graham crackers			grapes
cereal			
apples			
baby carrots			
celery sticks			

Source: *Sports Nutrition : A Guide for the Professional Working with Active People,* The American Dietetic Association.

Fluid Facts for Thirsty Young Athletes

Active kids need plenty of fluids. Grade school children are especially susceptible to heat exhaustion and heat stroke because they do not produce sweat as easily as adults. In addition, children gain heat faster from their surroundings because they have a greater body surface area in respect to their body weight. As a result, your child's body temperature will rise faster, and he can become dehydrated quickly.

Encourage your child to drink plenty of fluids. Keep a close watch, and make sure he is drinking something before, during, and after practices or games even though he may not feel thirsty. Children often fail to recognize or respond to the symptoms of thirst (see chart below).

Here are a few strategies to keep your child hydrated:

- Always send your child out the door with a sports bottle filled with fresh water.
- Make sure there's a cooler of cold water or sports drinks handy for events lasting more than one hour.
- Talk to your child's coach, and encourage her to schedule frequent "fluid breaks," especially in hot weather.

Fluid Guidelines for Active Kids

Before the Activity	During the Activity	After the Activity
Drink 10 to 14 ounces 1 to 2 hours before the activity.	Drink 3 to 4 ounces every 15 minutes.	Drink at least 16 ounces for every pound of weight lost. (Weigh your child before and after an event or practice.)

Chart adapted from *Play Hard, Eat Right*, American Dietetic Association, 1995.

Choosing the Right Fluids

When it comes to quenching your active child's thirst, all beverages are not created equal. Here are a few pointers to help you select the best beverages for your grade-schooler.

Water works best. Water is by far the best beverage for keeping your child hydrated. It's convenient and economical and refreshing when served cold. What's the best type of water to offer your child, tap or bottled? It really boils down to taste, because both types of water are regulated by government and are safe to drink.

Know the score on sports drinks. Most sports drinks contain a combination of water, carbohydrates, and the electrolytes sodium and potassium, which help regulate the body's water level. Though children can get plenty of fluid from drinking cold water and derive nutrients like sodium and potassium from foods in their daily diet, there's some evidence to suggest that kids who drink sports drinks are less likely to become dehydrated than kids who drink only water. That's because kids like the taste of sports drinks better, so they tend to drink more of it. If your child participates in all-day events or activities lasting longer than ninety minutes, sports drinks may be beneficial for carbohydrate replacement.

Look at the juicy details. Fruit juice is an okay choice before and after an activity. When selecting fruit juice, look for the ones labeled 100 percent juice. Fruit juice is not the best choice *during* sports events, though, because it is too rich in carbohydrates and may cause your child to have an upset stomach. If your child is more likely to drink a flavored beverage instead of water you can dilute the fruit juice: 1 cup of water for every cup of juice.

Forgo the fizz. While soft drinks are fine for kids to drink every once in a while, they're not the most thirst-quenching beverage. The carbonation may cause a burning sensation in your child's mouth, preventing her from gulping down enough fluid. And the high sugar content of regular soft drinks (one twelve-ounce can has nine teaspoons of sugar) can cause stomach cramps, nausea, and bloating if consumed quickly in large amounts. Finally, caffeinated soft drinks are actually dehydrating because the caffeine acts like a diuretic, causing your child to urinate more and lose even more fluid than she normally would.

WHAT TO EAT BEFORE COMPETITION

A pre-event meal is important to your child for two reasons. First, it can prevent her from feeling hungry before or during the activity. Second, it can supply her with enough energy and nutrients to go the distance. Skipping a meal before competition can impair performance by causing dizziness, fatigue, and even fainting spells.

For best results, a pre-event meal should be:

eaten three to four hours before competition.

high in complex carbohydrates. Some examples: pasta, cereal, or a baked potato.

low in fat and low to moderate in protein. A meal that is too high in fat and protein can sit undigested in the stomach and keep the blood from reaching working muscles. This can result in stomach cramping or nausea and a slower reaction time.

low in fiber and gas-producing foods. Foods like beans and high fiber salad or crackers may cause an upset stomach during the event.

Contrary to popular belief, foods that are high in sugar such as candy bars should be avoided before a sporting event. Sugar causes a sudden spike and then a sudden drop in blood-sugar levels. Instead of providing a quick energy boost, these foods cause athletes to start out in an energy slump. Most of the energy for exercise comes from foods that have been eaten several hours and even days prior to the event.

It's important to help your child make choices that work best for him. But if you have a child who prefers not to eat a meal before an event because he is nervous or excited, don't force the issue. Instead, encourage him to have a liquid meal like a glass of low-fat milk and a glass of juice.

Eating before the Event

1 to 2 Hours	2 to 3 Hours	3 or More Hours
Fruit or vegetable juice	Fruit or vegetable juice	Fruit or vegetable juice
Fresh fruit that is low in fiber such as plums, melon, and peaches	Fresh fruit	Fresh fruit
	Breads, bagels	Breads, bagels
	English muffins (without margarine or cream cheese)	English muffins
		Peanut butter, lean meat, low-fat cheese
		Low-fat yogurt
		Baked potato
		Cereal with low-fat milk
		Pasta with tomato sauce

Source: *Play Hard, Eat Right,* the American Dietetic Association, 1995.

WHAT TO EAT AFTER COMPETITION

As soon as your child is done with her activity or event, give her fluids for rehydration and complex carbohydrates to replenish glycogen stores (where the body stores energy for the next event). The body is most efficient at absorbing and storing energy (glycogen) during the first four to five hours after exercise. The postevent meal determines how much energy an athlete will have for the next training session or competition. Here are some examples of foods and fluids to give your child immediately after her activity:

medium-sized bagel
pretzel
low-fat yogurt
large banana

About two hours after exercising, your child should eat a meal that is rich in carbohydrates, such as spaghetti with meat sauce, Italian bread, green beans, strawberries, and low-fat milk.

TEACHING SMART NUTRITION TO YOUR YOUNG ATHLETE

The growing emphasis on winning and being number one has placed an overwhelming burden on young athletes. Even during the grade school years, kids may start to look for the competitive edge. At the same time, many of their sports heros advertise products such as amino acid supplements, protein powders, or vitamin and mineral packs. According to the American Academy of Pediatrics, high-performance supplements and weight-training programs to reduce body fat or increase muscle mass have no place in grade school athletics. It's your job to keep the lines of communication open with your child. Emphasize that the best way to get a jump start on doing the best they can is to eat a balanced diet and drink plenty of fluids. These habits may not create a bodybuilder or athletic champion overnight, but they will help your child grow strong and healthy.

SPORT SPECIFICS

Because different types of sports have different nutritional demands, we've come up with some common gradeschool sport scenerios and provided you with nutrition recommendations that will help fuel for maximum performance.

In for the Long Run

Chris, a sixth-grader, has joined an all-year swim team, which involves several all-day meets. His swimming events are usually scheduled about two to three hours apart. He often gets hungry between events but is afraid to eat a lot.

Sports-Nutrition Analysis. This scenario is common among sports that involve all-day events such as swimming, track, and gymnastics. The key is to keep your child sufficiently energized without feeding him too heavily between events. Drinking plenty of fluids is also important.

Here's what you can do:

- *The night before the event,* have your child eat a balanced dinner that is high in carbohydrates such as grilled chicken, a baked potato, green beans, fruit salad, and low-fat milk.
- *On the day of the event,* pack a small cooler with healthy foods and fluids. Bring foods that can be easily digested such as bagels, bananas, and oranges, cheese and crackers, low-fat granola bars, and pretzels.
- Have your child stay away from chips, greasy foods, and hot dogs.
- Have cold water and sports drinks readily available, and encourage your child to drink plenty of fluids throughout the day.

Fueled for High Intensity

Megan, a third-grader, has recently joined a soccer team. Her games are played early on Saturday mornings and are quite a distance from her house. She refuses to eat breakfast so early in the morning because it gives her an upset stomach.

Sports-Nutrition Analysis. High-intensity sports like soccer and basketball require a lot of energy, so it's important that growing children get enough calories, especially if they practice several times a week. Many kids have a hard time eating before an event, often because they're nervous or just not hungry. The key is not to force them to eat but to try to find something their stomachs can tolerate.

Here's what you can do:

- Plain bagels or a piece of fruit may work well. Or if your child just refuses to eat, encourage her to try a liquid meal.
- If you have to travel a distance to get to sports events, pack some snacks for the trip (see the Snacks to Pack Chart, page 180).
- Encourage your child to drink fluids before, during, and after the game.
- Make sure to pack a snack for the long ride home to help your child replenish her glycogen stores. An example of a nutritious snack that is high in carbohydrates: raisins, graham crackers, or yogurt.
- Grab a water bottle or sports drink to make sure that your child drinks enough fluids after the event.

Bulking Up

Christopher, a fifth-grader, is excited about starting football practice. But he has told his mom that he would like to add some more muscle before practice begins.

Sports-Nutrition Analysis. Kids who want to tackle on a football team or be a power hitter in baseball are often looking for ways to become stronger. During the grade school years, some boys may be starting puberty, which would enable them to add muscle more quickly than boys who have not yet entered puberty. It's important to talk with your child and stress that all kids—boys and girls—develop at different rates.

Here's what you can do:

- Emphasize the importance of eating a balanced diet and discourage your child from using protein supplements to add muscle. Explain that there is no scientific evidence to suggest that young athletes benefit from adding protein to their diet, and that more protein will build bigger muscles.
- Make sure your child is drinking plenty of fluids, especially when it's hot outside. Football and hockey players, in particular, wear protective gear, which reduces their body's ability to cool off.
- Encourage coaches to schedule regular fluid breaks. And make sure to send your child off to practice with a water bottle.

Weighty Issues

Jenna, a second-grader, has been on a gymnastics team for two years. Recently, she has mentioned that she wants to lose weight. She refuses to eat lunch and only eats an apple before she goes to practice after school.

Sports-Nutrition Analysis. In sports like gymnastics, figure skating, and wrestling, where appearance and weight are judged, many young athletes restrict their food or fluid intake in hopes of improving their scores. Stay involved and help your child keep a healthy perspective. Here's what you can do:

- Emphasize how important good nutrition is for proper growth. Take time to review the Food Guide Pyramid with your child and discuss how much she should eat each day to meet her nutritional needs.
- Stress how beautiful and strong your child is and how well she is doing in her sport.
- Talk with your child's coach to find out if he is putting pressure on her to lose weight.
- If weight continues to be an issue, talk with your pediatrician, and seek out the services of a registered dietitian.

Family Fitness Plan

We've already discussed how important it is to plan ahead for healthy meals, but taking the time to plan for physical activity is just as important. Developing a family fitness plan is a good way to get your child involved and make fitness a priority. Depending on your family schedule, you can plan a week's or month's worth of activities at a time.

Here are some steps you can take to get started.

1. Call your family together for a discussion.
2. Ask family members to suggest some of their favorite activities, such as
   - taking a family hike in the forest preserve;
   - riding bikes to the library after dinner;
   - going for a family swim at the local YMCA.
3. Let everyone select at least one activity they'd like the family to try. Then ask the following questions to determine the feasibility of your plan.

   - Do we all have enough time for this activity?
   - How much money can we spend?
   - Is the activity in a convenient location?
   - Is everyone able to participate in this type of activity?
   - Is it fun?
4. Develop your plan. Write down your ideas on a family calendar, or be creative and develop a calendar just for fitness.
5. Get moving!

CHAPTER 10

Red Flags

◆ ◆ ◆

I can't eat peanuts because they will make me sick.
—CHRISTIAN, FIRST GRADE

I look so fat in that dress.
—ERICA, THIRD GRADE

Can I become a vegetarian?
—ADAM, FIFTH GRADE

Top Three Mistakes Parents Make When It Comes to Their Children's Nutrition Health:

1. They put them on "diets."
2. They let them eat too much fat, especially saturated fat.
3. They think certain foods will influence their behavior.

As we discussed in the Introduction, our goal in writing this book is to give parents the nutritional knowledge and practical skills to teach their grade school child how to eat smart in and out of the classroom. We realize, though, that many parents also have to deal with nutrition and health issues like weight problems, high blood pressure, and food allergies. That's why we included this chapter on red flags. Based on our experience as registered dietitians and mothers of grade-schoolers, we've compiled the most common questions we receive from concerned parents, along with answers based on current nutrition recommendations and suggestions on where you can turn for additional help.

ANSWERS TO QUESTIONS COMMONLY ASKED BY PARENTS OF GRADE-SCHOOLERS

How can I tell if my child is overweight?

Since kids grow in unpredictable growth spurts, it can be very difficult to determine if a child is overweight simply by looking at him. For example, it's perfectly normal for grade school boys to have a growth spurt in weight, then catch up later in height. Talk with your pediatrician if you think your child is overweight. Pediatricians can assess your child's weight most accurately because they keep an annual record of your child's height and weight on standardized growth charts (see Appendix B). These charts can indicate whether a child falls within the normal range of height and weight for his age and can also plot weight against height independent of age.

Your pediatrician can also determine your child's body mass index (BMI). This is a calculation of a child's weight relative to height. For adults, a BMI above 27 indicates obesity. For children, standardized percentile curves have been developed to interpret BMI (see Appendix B). A BMI above the 95th percentile usually suggests that a child may have a weight problem.

What types of weight-loss diets are safe for my child?

Dieting is not recommended for children because they need calories to grow and develop properly. If your pediatrician determines that your child is overweight, he can help you start to make changes in your family's eating and activity habits. You can also look for a registered dietitian in your area who specializes in children's nutrition and who can develop an eating plan tailored to your family's lifestyle.

The best strategy for helping your child achieve a healthy weight is to teach him how to eat healthfully and be more physically active. Here are some proven ways to help kids control their weight:

- Plan your child's meals to include a variety of foods from each of the five food groups. Try to serve lower-fat and lower-sugar options from each group, such as a whole-wheat bagel instead of a doughnut; baked potato instead of french fries; 100 percent fruit juice instead of a fruit drink; and low-fat yogurt instead of regular yogurt. Also, serve foods such as candy, soda, and fruit drinks in moderation, and only after your child has eaten a selection from each of the food groups (see Chapter 2).
- Encourage your child to be physically active for at least sixty minutes every day (see Chapter 9).
- Be a role model, and let your kids see you eating healthy foods and being physically active. Chances are they will follow your example.
- Take time to talk to your child about his weight and ask him to discuss his feelings. Overweight children need support, acceptance, and encouragement from their family.

Should my child take nutritional supplements?

According to the American Academy of Pediatrics, most healthy children do not need nutritional supplements. Therefore the question of whether or not to give your child a multivitamin or mineral supplement is one you should discuss with your pediatrician. Large doses of vitamins and minerals such as vitamin A and iron can be dangerous if taken in excess. Children generally need supplements only under the following circumstances:

- If fluoride is lacking in the home water supply
- If a child cannot properly absorb the fats in his diet
- If a child is on a strict vegetarian diet
- If a child has a special medical condition such as anemia, which requires an iron supplement

In addition to vitamin and mineral supplements, there are high-calorie and high-protein products on the market. If you are concerned that your child is underweight, you should talk to your pediatrician to help determine if a problem exists before trying these products. Remember, growth and weight gain vary widely in children. Since your pediatrician will monitor your child's growth on standardized charts over time, she can determine if your child is growing at an acceptable rate.

How can I tell if my child is developing an eating disorder?

This question is becoming much more common among parents of grade school children. Alarming statistics have indicated that about 30 to 50 percent of eight- to nine-year-old American girls report feeling "too fat," and 20 to 40 percent are dieting. The problem becomes even more prevalent among adolescent girls. Research has estimated that more than 50 percent of fourteen-year-old girls have dieted during the eighth-grade year. Our society's emphasis on thinness and preoccupation with dieting has definitely had an influence on children and adolescents—particularly girls.

There is still no clear understanding of why a child (or teen) develops an eating disorder such as anorexia nervosa or bulimia nervosa. Although an eating disorder usually starts with a weight-loss diet and a desire to change one's body image, it's a much more complex disease. Eating disorders usually involve physical, psychological, and family components.

Talk with your pediatrician if your child shows any of the following signs of an eating disorder.

Common Eating Disorders

Anorexia nervosa is a disorder in which preoccupation with dieting and thinness leads to excessive weight loss. Common warning signs include:

- loss of a significant amount of weight
- intense fear of gaining weight
- preoccupation with food, calories, and fat
- lying about food
- loss of menstrual period
- depression or anxiety
- physical symptoms such as cold hands and feet, fainting spells, or hair loss.

Bulimia is a disorder in which frequent episodes of binge eating are followed by vomiting. Common warning signs include:

- binging or eating uncontrollably
- purging by strict dieting, fasting, vigorous exercise, vomiting, or use of laxatives
- using the bathroom frequently after meals
- preoccupation with body weight
- depression or mood swings
- physical symptoms such as dental problems, sore throat, or irregular periods.

Source: The National Eating Disorder Association.

How can I help my child like her body?

Even though many young girls or boys who diet will never develop an eating disorder, it is very important to stay involved and help your child develop a healthy body image. According to Anorexia Nervosa and Related Eating Disorders, Inc., a national organization specializing in helping individuals with an eating disorder, "Eating disorders are much easier to prevent than cure."

Here are some suggestions to help you guide your child toward developing a healthy attitude about her body and toward eating:

- Give her the gift of being a healthy role model yourself. Make healthy eating and physical activity a part of your lifestyle. In addition, try never to criticize your physical appearance or the appearance of others.
- Stress that healthy bodies come in all shapes and sizes, and that no one body shape or body size is a healthy one, or the right one, for everybody.
- Emphasize the importance of good nutrition in developing a healthy body. Help your child learn to be responsible for what, and how much, she eats.
- Gather your family together for at least one meal each day. Try to keep this time positive, social, and fun.
- Encourage your child to be active and feel good about all the things she can do. Help her find an activity that she feels comfortable in doing and enjoys.
- Be patient, and keep communicating with your child about any problems or concerns.

Should I have my child's cholesterol tested?

According to the American Heart Association and the National Cholesterol Education Program's expert panel, routine cholesterol testing of all children is unnecessary. The only reason to have your child's blood cholesterol tested is if:

- a parent or grandparent has had a history of heart problems or has been diagnosed with blocked arteries or a disease affecting the blood vessels, such as stroke, before the age of fifty-five;
- one parent has high cholesterol (240 milligrams per deciliter or higher);

• one parent's medical history is not known. This is especially important if the child has other risk factors for heart disease such as high blood pressure, obesity, diabetes, or physical inactivity.

If there is a history of heart disease and/or high blood cholesterol in your family, it's important to let your pediatrician know. Early identification and treatment of children and adolescents with high cholesterol levels may reduce their risk for developing heart disease later in life.

What should I do if my child has high cholesterol?

Children who are tested and found to have high blood cholesterol should be under the supervision of their pediatrician and registered dietitian. They need to have their blood cholesterol, eating behaviors, and risk factors such as high blood pressure, obesity, and diabetes monitored regularly. Your pediatrician will probably also want to complete a fasting lipoprotein test to measure HDL cholesterol and LDL cholesterol levels. Lipoproteins are protein-coated "packages" that carry fat in the bloodstream. High-density lipoproteins (HDLs)—or "good" blood cholesterol—take cholesterol away from the blood and arteries. Low-density lipoproteins (LDLs)—or "bad" blood cholesterol—keep cholesterol in your bloodstream.

When a child has high cholesterol, the preferred course of treatment is to make lifestyle changes such as switching to a low-cholesterol, low-fat diet and getting more physical activity. Your pediatrician will probably recommend the Step 1 diet from the American Heart Association. This balanced, healthy diet alters the fat content of every meal so that it is consistent with the fat, saturated fat, and cholesterol guidelines determined by cardiovascular and nutrition experts. This diet is healthy for the whole family. In fact, the calorie and fat recommendations in the Step 1 diet are consistent with those that the American Heart Association prescribes for all children over the age of two.

How much fat should my grade-schooler eat?

That depends on her daily calorie needs, which vary from child to child. The American Heart Association and the Dietary Guidelines (see Chapter 2) recommend that no more than 30 percent of your child's daily calories come from fat, and fewer than 10 percent of those calories from saturated fat. What's more, your child's diet should contain no more than three hundred milligrams of cholesterol (see "What Foods Contain Cholesterol?" chart below).

What Foods Contain Cholesterol?

Cholesterol is found only in animal products. Meat, poultry, seafood, dairy products, egg yolks, organ meats, and animal fats such as butter and lard all supply cholesterol in varying amounts. Check out how much cholesterol is in the following foods:

Beef liver (3 ounces)	301 milligrams
Egg yolk (1)	213 milligrams
Shrimp (8, large)	94 milligrams
Hamburger (3 ounces)	74 milligrams
Chicken, white and dark meat (3 ounces)	76 milligrams
Butter (1 tablespoon)	31 milligrams
Hot dog (1)	23 milligrams

Source: Nutrient data from the *Food Processor* 7.7 edition, ESHA Research 2001.

How can you use these guidelines? You can estimate your child's recommended fat intake by multiplying the number of calories he needs each day by 30 percent to determine how many calories should come from fat. For saturated fat, multiply by 10 percent. For example, in a two thousand-calorie diet, about six hundred calories should come from fat and fewer than two hundred calories from saturated fat.

You can use the chart below to translate these recommendations into daily fat and saturated fat grams (all fat contains nine calories per gram). The calories listed are based on the average calorie needs for different ages. It's important to note that calorie needs vary from child to child, depending on their size, growth rate, and level of physical activity.

Calorie and Fat Goals: What to Aim For

Age	Daily Calories	Total Fat Grams	Saturated Fat Grams
4–6	1,800	60	20
7–10	2,000	66	22
11–12 (girls)	2,200	73	24
11–12 (boys)	2,500	83	28

Here are a few strategies to help you fit these guidelines into your child's diet.

- Use the Nutrition Facts Label to help choose foods that are lower in fat, saturated fat, and cholesterol (see Chapter 8).
- Choose fat-free or low-fat dairy products (see Chapter 2).
- Eat fast foods in moderation, and look for the lowest-fat options (see Chapter 7).
- Buy lean cuts of meat such as sirloin, flank steak, or lean ground beef. Trim excess fat, and cook using fat-reducing methods like grilling or broiling (see Chapter 5).

Can too much salt cause my child to get high blood pressure?

Hypertension, or high blood pressure, can begin in childhood, especially in children who are overweight and have a family history of the disease. Other risk factors include physical inactivity, consumption of alcohol, cigarette smoking, and, for some a high sodium (salt) intake. It is estimated that about 30 percent of people in America are considered to be "sodium sensitive." For these individuals, too much sodium in the diet may contribute to high blood pressure. Other nutrients may also affect high blood pressure.

Who should limit their sodium intake?

Because there is no simple way to screen for sodium sensitivity, the National Heart, Lung, and Blood Institute recommends that children with high blood pressure follow a moderate sodium-restricted diet in which they have no more than 1,500 to 2,400 milligrams a day. In addition, the National Research Council recommends that *everyone* over the age of two try to consume no more than 2,400 milligrams of sodium daily. One teaspoon of salt contains about 2,300 milligrams of sodium daily. If you are concerned that your child has one or more of the risk factors for developing high blood pressure, talk with your pediatrician.

In addition, here are some healthy lifestyle strategies to help keep your child's blood pressure under control.

- Have her eat a balanced diet based on the Food Guide Pyramid. Include lots of fruits and vegetables and low-fat dairy products in her meals (see Chapter 2).
- Encourage her to be physically active every day (see Chapter 9).
- Make simple changes in your family lifestyle to reduce sodium intake, like keeping the salt shaker off the table and limiting trips to fast-food restaurants (see Chapter 7).

Is a vegetarian diet okay for my child?

Both the American Academy of Pediatrics and the American Dietetic Association feel that a carefully planned vegetarian diet can be nutritionally adequate for children. However, a vegetarian diet, like any other, has the potential to be healthful or unhealthful depending upon the food choices you make. Here are a few important things to keep in mind.

- *When it comes to vegetarians, not all are created equal.* Even though all vegetarians eat grains, vegetables, and fruits, their diets vary considerably when it comes to animal products, which can alter the nutritional quality of the diet. For example, semivegetarians exclude red meat and sometimes poultry from their diet, but do include seafood, eggs, and dairy products. Vegans, the strictest of vegetarians, exclude all animal products. Vegetarian children who eat a small amount of meat, dairy products, and/or eggs will probably get enough of the protein and other nutrients they need. But if your child is a vegan who excludes meat, poultry, seafood, dairy products and eggs, you'll want to make sure he gets adequate amounts of vitamin B_{12}, calcium, vitamin D, iron, and zinc, which are found mostly in these foods. For example, since vitamin B_{12} is found only in animal-based foods, you'll need to purchase foods that have been fortified with vitamin B_{12} such as breakfast cereal, breads, and soy milk. Or you can talk to your pediatrician about a vitamin B_{12} supplement. In addition, dairy products provide the majority of calcium in the diet, so you will need to encourage your child to consume a variety of calcium-fortified foods.
- *Calories should be your key concern.* Studies have shown that vegetarians no longer need to combine specific foods within a particular meal to make complete proteins. Your child's body will make its own complete proteins if she consumes a variety of plant foods and/or dairy products and enough total calories throughout the day. In fact, calories are even more important than protein when it comes to your child's growth. But because vegetarian diets tend to contain complex carbohydrates and

high fiber from foods such as whole-grain cereals and bread, fruits, and vegetables, they can be "bulkier" and more filing than regular diets. This can be a problem if your child fills up on high-fiber foods before their calorie needs are met. To prevent this from happening, make sure your child eats high-calorie, nutrient-rich foods like peanut butter, nuts, seeds, and cheese.

I think my child is lactose intolerant. Does this mean he can't have milk?

Not necessarily. Your child may still be able to tolerate up to two cups of milk each day. But before you start cutting back on the amount of milk or dairy products your child includes in his diet, talk with your pediatrician. She can run tests to determine if he is actually lactose intolerant. In addition, your pediatrician can:

- determine if your child is having problems because of a specific food or possibly some other medical condition,
- distinguish between a food allergy and a food intolerance (see chart below),
- provide you with the needed resources, if your child is diagnosed with a food allergy or intolerance.

Your pediatrician may also refer you to a registered dietitian, who can help you and your child develop an eating plan that excludes problem foods without sacrificing nutrition.

Food Allergy vs. Food Intolerance

A *food allergy* is the immune system's abnormal response to a food that the body identifies as a harmful invader. When the food, referred to as an allergen, is eaten, chemicals are released, triggering allergy symptoms. Some common symptoms of a food allergy include vomiting, abdominal pain, diarrhea, hives, rash, eczema, runny nose, labored breathing, and possibly a temporary drop in blood pressure. The most common food allergens are:

- eggs
- fish
- milk
- peanuts
- shellfish (shrimp, crab, and lobster)
- soy (found in soy beans, soy milk, and tofu)
- tree nuts (almonds, pecans, cashews, Brazil nuts, and walnuts)
- wheat

A food intolerance is a food-induced reaction that does not involve the immune system. For instance, a person with lactose intolerance lacks the enzyme lactase, that is needed to digest milk sugar. When the person eats any type of milk products, he may experience symptoms such as gas, bloating, and abdominal pain.

While people with a food allergy must completely avoid an offending food, people with a food intolerance can often eat some of the offending food without significant side effects. For example, some people with lactose intolerance can drink up to two cups of milk each day. In addition, they can use lactase enzymes tablets to help digest lactose in milk and milk products.

Source: The Food Allergy and Anaphylaxis Network

How can I make sure my child will not be served a food she is allergic to when she is away from home?

If your child has been diagnosed with a food allergy, you know how important it is for her to avoid any products that are made with the allergen. This can be a challenge, especially as your grade-schooler becomes more independent. The most important thing, though, is to teach your child about her food allergy and make her aware of all the foods she needs to avoid. There are several kid-friendly resources available from the Food Allergy Network, including a newsletter and on-line activities (see resources at the end of this chapter).

Here are a few additional strategies to follow.

- Talk with school officials about your child's allergies. Be sure to specify which foods need to be avoided. Food-service staff can provide you with school lunch menus along with a list of specific ingredients so you and your child can select safe foods to order.
- When eating out, ask about ingredients and preparation methods before you order.
- Try to review the menu before you try a new restaurant so you can make sure there is something for your child to eat.
- If your child is invited to a friend's house, call ahead and tell a parent about his food allergy. Provide her with a list of possible snacks, or offer to have your child bring a treat.

Are there special diets for kids with ADHD?

The American Academy of Pediatrics does not recommend special diets for the treatment of attention deficit/hyperactivity disorder. Special diets for the treatment of ADHD, such as the Feingold diet, have surfaced over the years, and are based on the theory that allergies or reactions to foods can cause hyperactivity. These diets have focused on artificial food additives, sugar, or common food allergies like corn or nuts. At this time, however, it has not been shown that dietary intervention offers significant help to children with learning and attention problems.

The current recommended treatment for ADHD is behavior modification, and medication if needed. Experts recommend that parents of children with ADHD:

- seek up-to-date, *scientific* information and professional help when needed,
- provide their child with clear, consistent guidelines, and work as a family to reinforce these guidelines,
- identify their child's strengths and build upon them.

Can the hormones in milk lead to the early onset of puberty?

Several studies have been published in *Pediatrics* and other leading medical journals regarding "precocious" or early-onset puberty. These articles discuss studies that have found that some girls may be starting to show signs of puberty, such as breast and pubic hair development, earlier (approximately one year earlier for white girls and two years earlier in African American girls) than was reported in the past. The verdict is still out, though, as to why the beginning signs of puberty are showing up earlier than in the past. Some possible theories include improved diet, increased weight, and decreased physical activity (see Chapter 9).

Increased weight is one of the leading theories, because childhood obesity has doubled in the past twenty years and body fat triggers hormones. One study published in the *American Journal of Public Health* found that girls who begin menstruating before age eleven are more likely to be overweight than girls who get their periods later.

There is currently no scientific evidence to indicate that the hormone bovine somotropin (BST), given to cows to increase milk production, plays a role in early-onset puberty. BST is a naturally occurring hormone made by cows. It is *normally* found in cow's milk and meat in small amounts. BST can also be given to cows as a supplement to improve their milk production. With BST supplementation, a cow's milk production goes up, but the actual level of BST in the milk does not change. There's no change in the flavor or nutritional quality of the milk, either. In 1990, the National Institutes of Health reinforced the safety of BST for humans. In 1993, the Food and Drug Administration approved BST supplementation, stating that the hormone is safe for human consumption—even in the increased amounts given to cows. And regulatory agencies in twenty countries since have authorized milk and meat from cows receiving BST as safe for people of all ages.

Talk with your pediatrician about any concerns you may have regarding your child's growth and development.

Does eating too much chocolate and fried foods cause acne?

Although acne is usually a problem that teenagers have to deal with, some grade-schoolers who are experiencing signs of puberty may start to get acne. Is it because they're eating foods like chocolate, potato chips, and candy? Contrary to popular belief, acne is linked to hormonal changes in the body, and rarely to food. Hormones whose levels rise during puberty can stimulate and enlarge the oil glands of the skin. These glands are found in areas where acne is usually a problem, such as on the face, upper back, and chest.

The best way for your child to keep his skin healthy is to eat an overall balanced diet (see Chapter 2), keep his skin clean, get enough rest—and wait. After the body matures, most cases of acne clear up. If problems are severe or persist, talk to your pediatrician or a dermatologist about future treatment.

What causes cavities?

A cavity forms when bacteria in the mouth (found in dental plaque) mixes with carbohydrates (from either sugary or starchy foods like crackers, popcorn, bread, and potato chips) to make acids. These acids eat away at tooth enamel, causing cavities. The more often your child eats foods that contain sugar and starches, and the longer these foods remain in his mouth before he brushes his teeth, the greater his risk for tooth decay.

Some carbohydrates, such as sugar and sweets, are more likely to cause tooth decay than others. In addition, foods such as hard candy, chewing gum, cookies, and granola bars take a while to dissolve and provide more time for the acids to cause damage to the teeth.

Here are some tips on how to combat cavities in your grade-schooler.

- Promote good dental habits. Encourage your child to brush her teeth with a fluoride toothpaste at least twice a day—preferably between meals and snacks—and to floss daily. You should also make sure that your child visits a pediatric dentist regularly.

- Eat a nutritious and balanced diet (see Chapter 2) and limit snacking to two to three times each day (see Chapter 6).
- Offer teeth-friendly foods. Foods like sharp cheddar, Monterey Jack, and Swiss cheese have been shown to increase the flow of saliva, which helps lower the acid levels in the mouth and prevent cavities. Plus they're excellent sources of calcium and phosphorous—nutrients that can make teeth healthy.

Should my child avoid certain foods now that she has braces?

Some foods can damage braces by pulling, bending, or breaking them. So your child should try to avoid sticky, gooey, crunchy, and hard foods. For example, caramel, taffy, and peanut brittle can stick to braces and pull them off your child's teeth. Foods like raw carrots, apples, hard candy, and corn chips can actually break the braces. Ask your child's orthodontist for a complete list of foods that might damage your child's braces.

Here are a few other tips to help your child keep her braces intact.

- Select soft fruits and vegetables like a banana or ripe peach, instead of an apple. Eat cucumber sticks instead of a whole raw carrot.
- Cut foods that require a lot of chewing into small pieces.
- Rinse your mouth with water after consuming sugary foods like candy and soda, before cavity-causing bacteria reaches the sugar.
- Stay away from gum. Gum can get caught on braces and pull them off. Also, the sugar in gum can get trapped behind braces and cause cavities.

Are herbal supplements safe for my child?

Although herbal remedies have been around since ancient times, there has definitely been a renewed interest in them in recent years. But before you give your child herbal supplements, there are a few things you should know.

1. Herbs and plants have chemical structures, and, like any chemical, can have an effect on the body. It is still unclear, however, whether some herbs provide medical benefits—and in what amounts.
2. Because herbal supplements are regulated as foods by the Food and Drug Administration, they don't have to meet the same strict guidelines that are required for drugs.
3. Because herbal supplements are made from plants, they don't always contain standard amounts of active ingredients. In addition, some manufacturers are more careful than others in removing other substances contained in the plant.
4. Herbs have not been tested on children, and there are *no* established medical guidelines for determining proper dosage for kids.

Talk with your pediatrician or registered dietitian about the safety of an herbal supplement before giving it to your child.

EXTRA-CREDIT ASSIGNMENT

For More Information...

The following organizations can provide you with more information about topics covered in this chapter. Contact those that
are of interest to you.

American Academy of Pediatrics
141 North West Point Boulevard
P.O. Box 927
Elk Grove Village, IL 60009-0927
847-228-5005
www.aap.org

American Dental Association
211 East Chicago Avenue
Chicago, IL 60611
312-444-2500
www.ada.org

American Dietetic Association
216 West Jackson Boulevard
Chicago, IL 60604
800-366-1655
www.eatright.org

The National Eating Disorder Association
165 West 46th Street, Suite 1108
New York, NY 10036
212-575-6200
www.edap.org

(continued)

For More Information . . . (continued)

American Heart Association
7320 Greenville Avenue
Dallas, TX 75231
214-373-6300
www.americanheart.org

National Association of Anorexia and Associated Disorders (ANAD)
P.O. Box 7
Highland Park, IL 60035
847-831-3436
www.anad.org

The Food Allergy and Anaphylaxis Network
4744 Holly Avenue
Fairfax, VA 22030-5647
1-800-929-4040
www.foodallergy.org

Appendix A

◆ ◆ ◆

Key Nutrients in Foods and How They Work in Your Child's Body

Major Nutrients	Functions	Food Sources
Carbohydrate	Supplies energy	Bread and cereal products, fruits, vegetables, milk and milk products
Protein	Builds and repairs all tissues Forms enzymes and hormones Forms antibodies to fight infection Supplies energy	Meat, fish, poultry, eggs, dairy products, dried beans, peas, peanut butter, nuts, and seeds
Fat	Concentrated energy source Suppplies essential fatty acids Carries fat-soluble vitamins	Butter, margarine, oil, meat, fish, poultry, cheese, eggs, nuts, and seeds
Minerals: Calcium	Forms and maintains bones and teeth Aids in blood clotting Aids in muscle movement and nerve transmission	Milk and milk products, sardines, kale, turnip greens, dried beans, fortified orange juice

Major Nutrients	Functions	Food Sources
Iron	Forms hemoglobin, which carries oxygen in the blood Helps release energy	Liver, meat, fish, poultry, eggs, dried beans, peas, nuts, green leafy vegetables, dried fruits, whole-grain or enriched breads and cereals
Zinc	Necessary for growth, healing, and formation of protein	Meat, liver, poultry, eggs, whole-grain breads and cereals, and milk
Fat-Soluble Vitamins:		
Vitamin A	Forms and maintains skin and mucus membranes Aids in vision, especially at night	Liver, egg yolks, butter, milk, dark green and deep yellow fruits and vegetables
Vitamin D	Helps body absorb calcium to build strong bones and teeth	Fortified milk, fish, liver oils
Vitamin E	Protects vitamins A and C from destruction by oxygen Prevents cell damage	Vegetable oil, margarine, green leafy vegetables, whole grains, egg yolks, liver, avocado, nuts, and wheat germ
Water-Soluble Vitamins:		
Vitamin C	Strengthens blood vessels Aids bone, teeth, and gum formation Enhances iron absorption Hastens wound healing	Oranges, grapefruit, lemons, limes, berries, melons, tomatoes, potatoes, peppers, broccoli, greens, and cabbage

Major Nutrients	Functions	Food Sources
Vitamin B_1 (Thiamin)	Releases energy from food Promotes normal appetite and healthy nervous system	Pork, liver, veal, dried beans, nuts, whole-grain or enriched breads and cereals
Vitamin B_2 (Riboflavin)	Releases energy from food Promotes healthy skin	Meat, liver, milk, cottage cheese, yogurt, leafy green vegetables, whole-grain or enriched breads and cereals
Niacin	Aids in carbohydrate metabolism and formation of fat Promotes healthy skin and nervous system	Liver, meat, fish, poultry, peanuts, milk, whole-grain or enriched breads and cereals
Folic Acid	Aids in protein metabolism Promotes red blood cell formation	Liver, legumes, green leafy vegetables, enriched breads and cereals

Appendix B

◆ ◆ ◆

GROWTH CHARTS

2 to 20 years: Boys
Body mass index-for-age percentiles

NAME _____

RECORD # _____

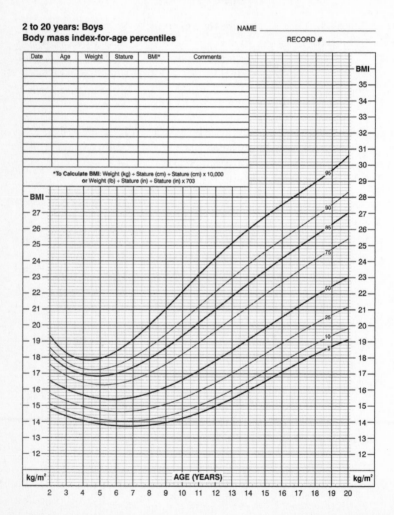

Boys Body mass index-for-age percentiles. Developed by the National Center for Health Statistics in collaboration with the National Center for Chronic Disease Prevention and Health Promotion (2000).   www.cdc.gov/growthcharts

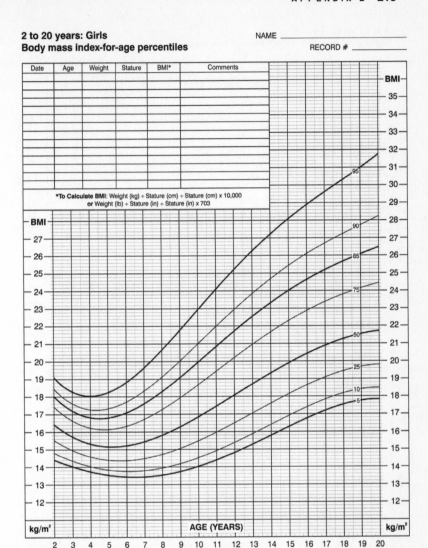

2 to 20 years: Girls
Body mass index-for-age percentiles

NAME _____

RECORD # _____

Date	Age	Weight	Stature	BMI*	Comments

*To Calculate BMI: Weight (kg) ÷ Stature (cm) ÷ Stature (cm) x 10,000
or Weight (lb) ÷ Stature (in) ÷ Stature (in) x 703

AGE (YEARS)

Girls Body mass index-for-age percentiles. Developed by the National Center for Health Statistics in collaboration with the National Center for Chronic Disease Prevention and Health Promotion (2000).   www.cdc.gov/growthcharts

2 to 20 years: Boys
Stature-for-age and Weight-for-age percentiles

NAME _____

RECORD # _____

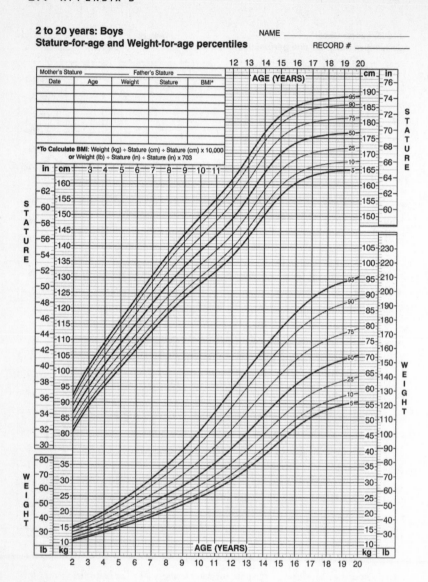

Boys Stature-for-age and Weight-for-age-percentiles. Developed by the National Center for Health Statistics in collaboration with the National Center for Chronic Disease Prevention and Health Promotion (2000).   www.cdc.gov/growthcharts

2 to 20 years: Girls
Stature-for-age and Weight-for-age percentiles

NAME _____

RECORD # _____

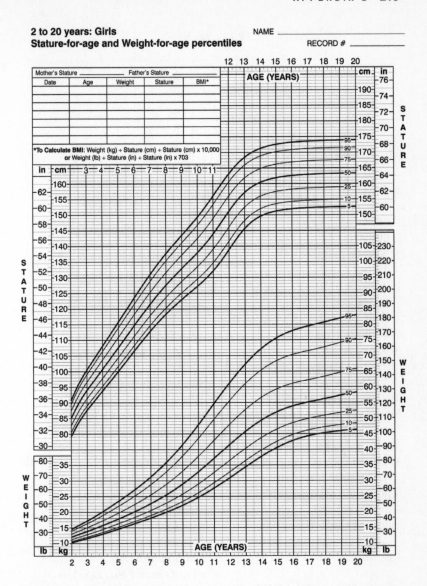

Girls Stature-for-age and Weight-for-age-percentiles. Developed by the National Center for Health Statistics in collaboration with the National Center for Chronic Disease Prevention and Health Promotion (2000).   www.cdc.gov/growthcharts

Index

◆ ◆ ◆

About the Authors

❖ ◆ ◆

Jodie Shield, M.Ed., R.D., has been a consultant and spokesperson in the field of nutrition for over a decade. A former national media spokesperson for the American Dietetic Association (1989–1995), she has worked extensively with the Rush-Presbyterian-St. Luke's Medical Center and taught nutrition and medical dietetics at the University of Illinois. Currently she is an associate complementary faculty member at Rush University in Chicago.

Jodie is senior partner at JM & Associates, a nutrition communications firm. Jodie has authored over two hundred articles for consumer magazines and professional journals such as *The Chicago Tribune, Ladies' Home Journal, Healthy Kids, American Baby, Shape Magazine's Fit Pregnancy, American Health,* and *Weight Watchers Magazine.* Currently she is the author of *Ask the Nutritionist* for Beansprout.net.

Jodie lives in the Chicago area with her husband and three grade school–age children, Jennifer, J.J., and Michael.

Mary Mullen, M.S. R.D., is senior partner at JM & Associates, a nutrition communications firm. She has coauthored several publications for the American Dietetic Association.

Mary is currently a pediatric outpatient dietition at Rush-Presbyterian-St. Luke's Medical Center, where she counsels children and adolescents on nutrition-related health issues. She also holds a faculty position in the Department of Nutrition. In addition, she has been the nutritionist for the Chicago White Sox for over ten years.

Mary is an active member of the American Dietetic Association and has held several leadership positions including delegate and president of the Illinois Dietetic Association. She lives in the Chicago area with her husband and four children, Joe, Kevin, Anne, and Maura.